The Comprehensive Air Fryer Cookbook UK

2000 Days of Crispy and Flavorful Recipes for Breakfast, Lunch, Dinner, Snacks, Desserts and More, Perfect for Air Fryer Beginners and Advanced Users

Ryan Devereaux

Copyright© 2023 By Ryan Devereaux
All rights reserved worldwide.

No part of this book may be reproduced or transmitted in any form or by any means, electronic or mechanical, including photo- copying, recording or by any information storage and retrieval system, without written permission from the publisher, except for the inclusion of brief quotations in a review.

Warning-Disclaimer

The purpose of this book is to educate and entertain. The author or publisher does not guarantee that anyone following the techniques, suggestions, tips, ideas, or strategies will become successful. The author and publisher shall have neither liability or responsibility to anyone with respect to any loss or damage caused, or alleged to be caused, directly or indirectly by the information contained in this book.

Table of Contents

01	Chapter 1	Breakfasts
10	Chapter 2	Family Favorites
14	Chapter 3	Fast and Easy Everyday Favourites
19	Chapter 4	Poultry
28	Chapter 5	Beef, Pork, and Lamb
38	Chapter 6	Fish and Seafood
48	Chapter 7	Snacks and Appetizers
57	Chapter 8	Vegetables and Sides
65	Chapter 9	Vegetarian Mains
69	Chapter 10	Desserts
76	Appendix : Recipe Index	

INTRODUCTION

Oh my goodness, have you heard about air fryers?! They're like magic wands for your kitchen! Hi, I'm the author of an Air Fryer Cookbook, and I'm so excited to share my love for air frying with you. This cookbook is perfect for anyone who wants to enjoy all the crispy goodness of fried food without any of the guilt.

With my cookbook, you'll learn how to make all sorts of delicious and healthy meals using your air fryer. From crispy chicken wings to buttery sweet potato, you'll be amazed at what you can cook up with this little wonder. And the best part? You'll save so much time and effort in the kitchen, you'll have more time to enjoy your yummy creations!

But wait, there's more! Air frying is also a healthier way to cook, so you can feel good about what you're putting into your body. Plus, with all the fun recipes in this cookbook, you'll never get bored with your meals again.

So, if you're ready to join the air fryer craze and become a foodie magician in your own kitchen, this cookbook is for you! Get ready to amaze your taste buds and your friends with your air frying skills.

Benefits of air frying

With this right-hand man, you can enjoy:

- **Healthier cooking:** Air frying uses significantly less oil than traditional frying methods, which can help you cook healthier meals. This can also lead to reduced calorie intake and lower fat consumption.
- **More convenience:** Air fryers are easy to use and require little to no preheating time. They also allow you to cook multiple dishes at once, which can help you save time in the kitchen.
- **Versatility:** Air fryers can cook a wide variety of foods, from chicken wings and french fries to vegetables and desserts. This means you can use your air fryer to make a range of meals and snacks.
- **Less mess:** Air fryers are less messy than traditional frying methods, which can help you keep your kitchen clean and tidy.
- **Better taste and texture:** Air frying can produce crispy, crunchy foods that are similar in taste and texture to traditional fried foods. This means you can enjoy the same delicious taste without the added calories and fat.

Tips for successful air frying

Hey! Before you try this, there are some tips for you to better use!

1. **Preheat the air fryer:** Preheating the air fryer can help ensure even cooking and crispy results.
2. **Don't overcrowd the basket:** Overcrowding the basket can prevent hot air from circulating properly and can lead to uneven cooking. It's better to cook in batches if needed.
3. **Use a light coating of oil:** While air frying uses less oil than traditional frying methods, a light coating of oil can help produce crispy and flavorful results.
4. **Shake the basket:** Shaking the basket during cooking can help ensure even cooking and prevent sticking.
5. **Check the food often:** Air fryers cook food quickly, so it's important to check the food often to avoid overcooking or burning.
6. **Experiment with cooking times and temperatures:** Different foods may require different cooking times and temperatures, so it's important to experiment to find what works best for each recipe.
7. **Clean the air fryer regularly:** Cleaning the air fryer after each use can help prevent buildup and ensure it continues to function properly.

Essential equipment and accessories

Except for tips we provide to you, there are essential equipment and accessories of the air fryer that you should know.

- **Accessory kit:** An accessory kit includes pans, racks, silicone molds, and everything else you need to maximize your air fryer
- **Air-fryer rack:** Racks add versatility to the air fryer and maximize surface cooking. Additionally, use the skewer rack for kabobs or other dishes

- **Air-fryer cookbook:** An air-fryer cookbook with over 100 recipes can help you cook every meal, plus snacks and desserts in your air fryer
- **Perforated silicone mats:** These mats are fantastic for keeping food from sticking on your air fryer basket or wire racks
- **Accessory kit:** Don't want to purchase everything separately? Get an air-fryer accessory kit that includes pans, racks, silicone molds, and everything else you'll need to maximize use of your air fryer
- **Reversible air fryer rack:** This dual-purpose accessory can function as a rack for your air fryer, allowing air to circulate
- **Liners:** Liners can help keep your air fryer clean and prevent food from sticking
- **Pizza pan:** A pizza pan can help you make crispy, delicious pizza in your air fryer
- **Skewers:** Skewers are great for making kabobs or other dishes in your air fryer
- **Muffin cups:** Muffin cups can be used to make muffins, cupcakes, or other baked goods in your air fryer
- **Cake pan:** A cake pan can be used to make cakes or other baked goods in your air fryer
- **Silicone mold:** A silicone mold can be used to make a variety of foods in your air fryer, such as egg bites or mini quiches
- **Instant Pot Air Fryer Lid:** If you already own an Instant Pot, you can purchase an Air Fryer Lid to turn it into an air fryer
- **Food thermometer:** A food thermometer can help ensure that your food is cooked to the proper temperature and prevent overcooking or undercooking

Safety Precautions and Maintenance

Safety Precautions:

1. Read the manual before using the air fryer to understand all the precautions you should take when using it

2. Use a silicone glove or oven-safe mitts to avoid burning yourself when touching hot components of the air fryer

3. Unplug the air fryer immediately after use to ensure that all heating components stay off and don't accidentally start up when you don't want them to

4. Never leave an in-use air fryer unattended, as food can burn quickly and cause a fire

Maintenance Tips:

1. Clean the air fryer regularly to prevent grease and food debris from accumulating. Most parts of an air fryer are dishwasher safe, but check the owner's manual for specific cleaning tips

2. Soak any parts with stuck-on food in hot water and dish detergent to loosen the food before cleaning

3. Use a wooden skewer or toothpick to poke out any food that may be stuck in the basket

4. Check regularly for signs of wear and tear, such as cracks or dents in components, particularly around areas where hot oil is used

Chapter 1

Breakfasts

Homemade Toaster Pastries

Prep time: 10 minutes | Cook time: 11 minutes | Makes 6 pastries

Oil, for spraying	340 g icing sugar
1 (425 g) package ready-to-roll pie crust	3 tablespoons milk
6 tablespoons jam or preserves of choice	1 to 2 tablespoons sprinkles of choice

1. Preheat the air fryer to 180°C. Line the air fryer basket with parchment and lightly spray with oil. 2. Cut the pie crust into 12 rectangles, about 3 by 4 inches each. You will need to reroll the dough scraps to get 12 rectangles. 3. Spread 1 tablespoon of jam in the centre of 6 rectangles, leaving ¼ inch around the edges. 4. Pour some water into a small bowl. Use your finger to moisten the edge of each rectangle. 5. Top each rectangle with another and use your fingers to press around the edges. Using the prongs of a fork, seal the edges of the dough and poke a few holes in the top of each one. Place the pastries in the prepared basket. 6. Air fry for 11 minutes. Let cool completely. 7. In a medium bowl, whisk together the icing sugar and milk. Spread the icing over the tops of the pastries and add sprinkles. Serve immediately.

Hole in One

Prep time: 5 minutes | Cook time: 6 to 7 minutes | Serves 1

1 slice bread	1 tablespoon grated Cheddar cheese
1 teaspoon soft butter	
1 egg	2 teaspoons diced gammon
Salt and pepper, to taste	

1. Place a baking dish inside air fryer basket and preheat the air fryer to 170°C. 2. Using a 2½-inch-diameter biscuit cutter, cut a hole in center of bread slice. 3. Spread softened butter on both sides of bread. 4. Lay bread slice in baking dish and crack egg into the hole. Sprinkle egg with salt and pepper to taste. 5. Cook for 5 minutes. 6. Turn toast over and top it with grated cheese and diced gammon. 7. Cook for 1 to 2 more minutes or until yolk is done to your liking.

Kale and Potato Nuggets

Prep time: 10 minutes | Cook time: 18 minutes | Serves 4

1 teaspoon extra virgin rapeseed oil	and mashed
	30 ml milk
1 clove garlic, minced	Salt and ground black pepper, to taste
1 kg kale, rinsed and chopped	
	Cooking spray
475 g potatoes, boiled	

1. Preheat the air fryer to 200°C. 2. In a skillet over medium heat, sauté the garlic in the rapeseed oil, until it turns golden brown. Sauté with the kale for an additional 3 minutes and remove from the heat. 3. Mix the mashed potatoes, kale and garlic in a bowl. Pour in the milk and sprinkle with salt and pepper. 4. Shape the mixture into nuggets and spritz with cooking spray. 5. Put in the air fryer basket and air fry for 15 minutes, flip the nuggets halfway through cooking to make sure the nuggets fry evenly. 6. Serve immediately.

Jalapeño and Bacon Breakfast Pizza

Prep time: 5 minutes | Cook time: 10 minutes | Serves 2

235 ml grated Cheddar cheese	chopped
	60 g chopped pickled jalapeños
30 g soft cheese, broken into small pieces	
	1 large egg, whisked
4 slices cooked bacon,	¼ teaspoon salt

1. Place Mozzarella in a single layer on the bottom of an ungreased round nonstick baking dish. Scatter soft cheese pieces, bacon, and jalapeños over Mozzarella, then pour egg evenly around baking dish. 2. Sprinkle with salt and place into air fryer basket. Adjust the temperature to 170°C and bake for 10 minutes. When cheese is brown and egg is set, pizza will be done. 3. Let cool on a large plate 5 minutes before serving.

Bourbon Vanilla French Toast

Prep time: 15 minutes | Cook time: 6 minutes | Serves 4

2 large eggs	2 tablespoons bourbon
2 tablespoons water	1 teaspoon vanilla extract
160 ml whole or semi-skimmed milk	8 (1-inch-thick) French bread slices
1 tablespoon butter, melted	Cooking spray

1. Preheat the air fryer to 160°C. Line the air fryer basket with parchment paper and spray it with cooking spray. 2. Beat the eggs with the water in a shallow bowl until combined. Add the milk, melted butter, bourbon, and vanilla and stir to mix well. 3. Dredge 4 slices of bread in the batter, turning to coat both sides evenly. Transfer the bread slices onto the parchment paper. 4. Bake for 6 minutes until nicely browned. Flip the slices halfway through the cooking time. 5. Remove from the basket to a plate and repeat with the remaining 4 slices of bread. 6. Serve warm.

Bacon and Spinach Egg Muffins

Prep time: 7 minutes | Cook time: 12 to 14 minutes | Serves 6

6 large eggs	180 g frozen chopped spinach, thawed and drained
60 ml double (whipping) cream	
½ teaspoon sea salt	4 strips cooked bacon, crumbled
¼ teaspoon freshly ground black pepper	60 g grated Cheddar cheese
¼ teaspoon cayenne pepper (optional)	

1. In a large bowl (with a spout if you have one), whisk together the eggs, double cream, salt, black pepper, and cayenne pepper (if using). 2. Divide the spinach and bacon among 6 silicone muffin cups. Place the muffin cups in your air fryer basket. 3. Divide the egg mixture among the muffin cups. Top with the cheese. 4. Set the air fryer to 150°C. Bake for 12 to 14 minutes, until the eggs are set and cooked through.

White Bean–Oat Waffles

Prep time: 10 minutes | Cook time: 20 minutes | Serves 2

1 large egg white	1 teaspoon coconut oil
2 tablespoons finely ground flaxseed	1 teaspoon liquid sweetener
120 ml water	120 g old-fashioned porridge oats
¼ teaspoon salt	
1 teaspoon vanilla extract	Extra-virgin rapeseed oil cooking spray
120 g cannellini beans, drained and rinsed	

1. In a blender, combine the egg white, flaxseed, water, salt, vanilla, cannellini beans, coconut oil, and sweetener. Blend on high for 90 seconds. 2. Add the oats. Blend for 1 minute more. 3. Preheat the waffle iron. The batter will thicken to the correct consistency while the waffle iron preheats. 4. Spray the heated waffle iron with cooking spray. 5. Add 180 ml batter. Close the waffle iron. Cook for 6 to 8 minutes, or until done. Repeated with the remaining batter. 6. Serve hot, with your favourite sugar-free topping.

Golden Avocado Tempura

Prep time: 5 minutes | Cook time: 10 minutes | Serves 4

60 g bread crumbs	peeled and sliced
½ teaspoons salt	Liquid from 1 can white beans
1 Haas avocado, pitted,	

1. Preheat the air fryer to 180°C. 2. Mix the bread crumbs and salt in a shallow bowl until well-incorporated. 3. Dip the avocado slices in the bean liquid, then into the bread crumbs. 4. Put the avocados in the air fryer, taking care not to overlap any slices, and air fry for 10 minutes, giving the basket a good shake at the halfway point. 5. Serve immediately.

Bacon Cheese Egg with Avocado

Prep time: 15 minutes | Cook time: 20 minutes | Serves 4

6 large eggs	peeled and pitted
60 ml double cream	8 tablespoons full-fat sour cream
350 g chopped cauliflower	2 spring onions, sliced on the bias
235 g grated medium Cheddar cheese	12 slices bacon, cooked and crumbled
1 medium avocado,	

1. In a medium bowl, whisk eggs and cream together. Pour into a round baking dish. 2. Add cauliflower and mix, then top with Cheddar. Place dish into the air fryer basket. 3. Adjust the temperature to 160ºC and set the timer for 20 minutes. 4. When completely cooked, eggs will be firm and cheese will be browned. Slice into four pieces. 5. Slice avocado and divide evenly among pieces. Top each piece with 2 tablespoons sour cream, sliced spring onions, and crumbled bacon.

Italian Egg Cups

Prep time: 5 minutes | Cook time: 10 minutes | Serves 4

rapeseed oil	Parmesan cheese
235 ml marinara sauce	Salt and freshly ground black pepper, to taste
4 eggs	
4 tablespoons grated Cheddar cheese	Chopped fresh basil, for garnish
4 teaspoons grated	

1. Lightly spray 4 individual ramekins with rapeseed oil. 2. Pour 60 ml marinara sauce into each ramekin. 3. Crack one egg into each ramekin on top of the marinara sauce. 4. Sprinkle 1 tablespoon of Mozzarella and 1 tablespoon of Parmesan on top of each egg. Season with salt and pepper. 5. Cover each ramekin with aluminum foil. Place two of the ramekins in the air fryer basket. 6. Air fry at 180ºC for 5 minutes and remove the aluminum foil. Air fry until the top is lightly browned and the egg white is cooked, another 2 to 4 minutes. If you prefer the yolk to be firmer, cook for 3 to 5 more minutes. 7. Repeat with the remaining two ramekins. Garnish with basil and serve.

Green Eggs and Ham

Prep time: 5 minutes | Cook time: 10 minutes | Serves 2

1 large Hass avocado, halved and pitted	½ teaspoon fine sea salt
2 thin slices ham	¼ teaspoon ground black pepper
2 large eggs	60 g grated Cheddar cheese (omit for dairy-free)
2 tablespoons chopped spring onions, plus more for garnish	

1. Preheat the air fryer to 200ºC. 2. Place a slice of ham into the cavity of each avocado half. Crack an egg on top of the ham, then sprinkle on the green onions, salt, and pepper. 3. Place the avocado halves in the air fryer cut side up and air fry for 10 minutes, or until the egg is cooked to your desired doneness. Top with the cheese (if using) and air fry for 30 seconds more, or until the cheese is melted. Garnish with chopped green onions. 4. Best served fresh. Store extras in an airtight container in the fridge for up to 4 days. Reheat in a preheated 180ºC air fryer for a few minutes, until warmed through.

Buffalo Egg Cups

Prep time: 10 minutes | Cook time: 15 minutes | Serves 2

4 large eggs	sauce
60 g full-fat soft cheese	120 g grated mature Cheddar cheese
2 tablespoons buffalo	

1. Crack eggs into two ramekins. 2. In a small microwave-safe bowl, mix soft cheese, buffalo sauce, and Cheddar. Microwave for 20 seconds and then stir. Place a spoonful into each ramekin on top of the eggs. 3. Place ramekins into the air fryer basket. 4. Adjust the temperature to 160ºC and bake for 15 minutes. 5. Serve warm.

Egg Tarts

Prep time: 10 minutes | Cook time: 17 to 20 minutes | Makes 2 tarts

⅓ sheet frozen puff pastry, thawed	2 eggs
Cooking oil spray	¼ teaspoon salt, divided
120 g grated Cheddar cheese	1 teaspoon minced fresh parsley (optional)

1. Insert the crisper plate into the basket and the basket into the unit. Preheat the unit by selecting BAKE, setting the temperature to 200ºC, and setting the time to 3 minutes. Select START/STOP to begin. 2. Lay the puff pastry sheet on a piece of parchment paper and cut it in half. 3. Once the unit is preheated, spray the crisper plate with cooking oil. Transfer the 2 squares of pastry to the basket, keeping them on the parchment paper. 4. Select BAKE, set the temperature to 200ºC, and set the time to 20 minutes. Select START/STOP to begin. 5. After 10 minutes, use a metal spoon to press down the center of each pastry square to make a well. Divide the cheese equally between the baked pastries. Carefully crack an egg on top of the cheese, and sprinkle each with the salt. Resume cooking for 7 to 10 minutes. 6. When the cooking is complete, the eggs will be cooked through. Sprinkle each with parsley (if using) and serve.

Strawberry Tarts

Prep time: 15 minutes | Cook time: 10 minutes | Serves 6

2 refrigerated piecrusts	yoghurt
120 g strawberry preserves	30 g soft cheese, at room temperature
1 teaspoon cornflour	3 tablespoons icing sugar
Cooking oil spray	Rainbow sprinkles, for decorating
120 ml low-fat vanilla	

1. Place the piecrusts on a flat surface. Using a knife or pizza cutter, cut each piecrust into 3 rectangles, for 6 total. Discard any unused dough from the piecrust edges. 2. In a small bowl, stir together the preserves and cornflour. Mix well, ensuring there are no lumps of cornflour remaining. 3. Scoop 1 tablespoon of the strawberry mixture onto the top half of each piece of piecrust. 4. Fold the bottom of each piece up to enclose the filling. Using the back of a fork, press along the edges of each tart to seal. 5. Insert the crisper plate into the basket and the basket into the unit. Preheat the unit by selecting BAKE, setting the temperature to 190ºC, and setting the time to 3 minutes. Select START/STOP to begin. 6. Once the unit is preheated, spray the crisper plate with cooking oil. Working in batches, spray the breakfast tarts with cooking oil and place them into the basket in a single layer. Do not stack the tarts. 7. Select BAKE, set the temperature to 190ºC, and set the time to 10 minutes. Select START/STOP to begin. 8. When the cooking is complete, the tarts should be light golden brown. Let the breakfast tarts cool fully before removing them from the basket. 9. Repeat steps 5, 6, 7, and 8 for the remaining breakfast tarts. 10. In a small bowl, stir together the yoghurt, soft cheese, and icing sugar. Spread the breakfast tarts with the frosting and top with sprinkles.

Egg in a Hole

Prep time: 5 minutes | Cook time: 5 minutes | Serves 1

1 slice bread	1 tablespoon grated Cheddar cheese
1 teaspoon butter, softened	2 teaspoons diced gammon
1 egg	
Salt and pepper, to taste	

1. Preheat the air fryer to 170ºC. Place a baking dish in the air fryer basket. 2. On a flat work surface, cut a hole in the center of the bread slice with a 2½-inch-diameter biscuit cutter. 3. Spread the butter evenly on each side of the bread slice and transfer to the baking dish. 4. Crack the egg into the hole and season as desired with salt and pepper. Scatter the grated cheese and diced gammon on top. 5. Bake in the preheated air fryer for 5 minutes until the bread is lightly browned and the egg is cooked to your preference. 6. Remove from the basket and serve hot.

Cheddar Soufflés

Prep time: 15 minutes | Cook time: 12 minutes | Serves 4

3 large eggs, whites and yolks separated	120 g grated mature Cheddar cheese
¼ teaspoon cream of tartar	85 g soft cheese, softened

1. In a large bowl, beat egg whites together with cream of tartar until soft peaks form, about 2 minutes. 2. In a separate medium bowl, beat egg yolks, Cheddar, and soft cheese together until frothy, about 1 minute. Add egg yolk mixture to whites, gently folding until combined. 3. Pour mixture evenly into four ramekins greased with cooking spray. Place ramekins into air fryer basket. Adjust the temperature to 180°C and bake for 12 minutes. Eggs will be browned on the top and firm in the center when done. Serve warm.

Potatoes Lyonnaise

Prep time: 10 minutes | Cook time: 31 minutes | Serves 4

1 sweet/mild onion, sliced	(about 450 g in total), sliced ½-inch thick
1 teaspoon butter, melted	1 tablespoon vegetable oil
1 teaspoon soft brown sugar	Salt and freshly ground black pepper, to taste
2 large white potatoes	

1. Preheat the air fryer to 190°C. 2. Toss the sliced onions, melted butter and soft brown sugar together in the air fryer basket. Air fry for 8 minutes, shaking the basket occasionally to help the onions cook evenly. 3. While the onions are cooking, bring a saucepan of salted water to a boil on the stovetop. Par-cook the potatoes in boiling water for 3 minutes. Drain the potatoes and pat them dry with a clean kitchen towel. 4. Add the potatoes to the onions in the air fryer basket and drizzle with vegetable oil. Toss to coat the potatoes with the oil and season with salt and freshly ground black pepper. 5. Increase the air fryer temperature to 200°C and air fry for 20 minutes, tossing the vegetables a few times during the cooking time to help the potatoes brown evenly. 6. Season with salt and freshly ground black pepper and serve warm.

Gyro Breakfast Patties with Tzatziki

Prep time: 10 minutes | Cook time: 20 minutes per batch | Makes 16

Patties:

900 g lamb or beef mince	1 teaspoon dried oregano leaves
120 g diced red onions	2 cloves garlic, minced
60 g sliced black olives	1 teaspoon fine sea salt
2 tablespoons tomato sauce	

Tzatziki:

235 ml full-fat sour cream	powder, or 1 clove garlic, minced
1 small cucumber, chopped	¼ teaspoon dried dill, or 1 teaspoon finely chopped fresh dill
½ teaspoon fine sea salt	
½ teaspoon garlic	

For Garnish/Serving:

120 g crumbled feta cheese (about 60 g)	Sliced black olives
Diced red onions	Sliced cucumbers

1. Preheat the air fryer to 180°C. 2. Place the lamb, onions, olives, tomato sauce, oregano, garlic, and salt in a large bowl. Mix well to combine the ingredients. 3. Using your hands, form the mixture into sixteen 3-inch patties. Place about 5 of the patties in the air fryer and air fry for 20 minutes, flipping halfway through. Remove the patties and place them on a serving platter. Repeat with the remaining patties. 4. While the patties cook, make the tzatziki: Place all the ingredients in a small bowl and stir well. Cover and store in the fridge until ready to serve. Garnish with ground black pepper before serving. 5. Serve the patties with a dollop of tzatziki, a sprinkle of crumbled feta cheese, diced red onions, sliced black olives, and sliced cucumbers. 6. Store leftovers in an airtight container in the refrigerator for up to 5 days or in the freezer for up to a month. Reheat the patties in a preheated 200°C air fryer for a few minutes, until warmed through.

Tomato and Cheddar Rolls

Prep time: 30 minutes | Cook time: 25 minutes | Makes 12 rolls

4 vine tomatoes	yeast
½ clove garlic, minced	2 teaspoons sugar
1 tablespoon rapeseed oil	2 teaspoons salt
¼ teaspoon dried thyme	1 tablespoon rapeseed oil
Salt and freshly ground black pepper, to taste	235 g grated Cheddar cheese, plus more for sprinkling at the end
500 g plain flour	350 ml water
1 teaspoon fast-action	

1. Cut the tomatoes in half, remove the seeds with your fingers and transfer to a bowl. Add the garlic, rapeseed oil, dried thyme, salt and freshly ground black pepper and toss well. 2. Preheat the air fryer to 200°C. 3. Place the tomatoes, cut side up in the air fryer basket and air fry for 10 minutes. The tomatoes should just start to brown. Shake the basket to redistribute the tomatoes, and air fry for another 5 to 10 minutes at 170°C until the tomatoes are no longer juicy. Let the tomatoes cool and then rough chop them. 4. Combine the flour, yeast, sugar and salt in the bowl of a stand mixer. Add the rapeseed oil, chopped roasted tomatoes and Cheddar cheese to the flour mixture and start to mix using the dough hook attachment. As you're mixing, add 300 ml of the water, mixing until the dough comes together. Continue to knead the dough with the dough hook for another 10 minutes, adding enough water to the dough to get it to the right consistency. 5. Transfer the dough to an oiled bowl, cover with a clean kitchen towel and let it rest and rise until it has doubled in volume, about 1 to 2 hours. Then, divide the dough into 12 equal portions. Roll each portion of dough into a ball. Lightly coat each dough ball with oil and let the dough balls rest and rise a second time, covered lightly with plastic wrap for 45 minutes. (Alternately, you can place the rolls in the refrigerator overnight and take them out 2 hours before you bake them.) 6. Preheat the air fryer to 180°C. 7. Spray the dough balls and the air fryer basket with a little rapeseed oil. Place three rolls at a time in the basket and bake for 10 minutes. Add a little grated Cheddar cheese on top of the rolls for the last 2 minutes of air frying for an attractive finish.

Spinach and Swiss Frittata with Mushrooms

Prep time: 10 minutes | Cook time: 20 minutes | Serves 4

rapeseed oil cooking spray	110 g baby mushrooms, sliced
8 large eggs	1 shallot, diced
½ teaspoon salt	120 g grated Swiss cheese, divided
½ teaspoon black pepper	Hot sauce, for serving (optional)
1 garlic clove, minced	
475 g fresh baby spinach	

1. Preheat the air fryer to 180°C. Lightly coat the inside of a 6-inch round cake pan with rapeseed oil cooking spray. 2. In a large bowl, beat the eggs, salt, pepper, and garlic for 1 to 2 minutes, or until well combined. 3. Fold in the spinach, mushrooms, shallot, and 60 ml the Swiss cheese. 4. Pour the egg mixture into the prepared cake pan, and sprinkle the remaining 60 ml Swiss over the top. 5. Place into the air fryer and bake for 18 to 20 minutes, or until the eggs are set in the center. 6. Remove from the air fryer and allow to cool for 5 minutes. Drizzle with hot sauce (if using) before serving.

Classic British Breakfast

Prep time: 5 minutes | Cook time: 25 minutes | Serves 2

235 g potatoes, sliced and diced	1 tablespoon rapeseed oil
475 g baked beans	1 sausage
2 eggs	Salt, to taste

1. Preheat the air fryer to 200°C and allow to warm. 2. Break the eggs onto a baking dish and sprinkle with salt. 3. Lay the beans on the dish, next to the eggs. 4. In a bowl, coat the potatoes with the rapeseed oil. Sprinkle with salt. 5. Transfer the bowl of potato slices to the air fryer and bake for 10 minutes. 6. Swap out the bowl of potatoes for the dish containing the eggs and beans. Bake for another 10 minutes. Cover the potatoes with parchment paper. 7. Slice up the sausage and throw the slices on top of the beans and eggs. Bake for another 5 minutes. 8. Serve with the potatoes.

Bacon, Broccoli and Cheese Bread Pudding

Prep time: 30 minutes | Cook time: 48 minutes | Serves 2 to 4

230 g streaky bacon, cut into ¼-inch pieces	freshly ground black pepper
700 g brioche bread or rolls, cut into ½-inch cubes	235 g frozen broccoli florets, thawed and chopped
3 eggs	350 g grated Emmental cheese
235 ml milk	
½ teaspoon salt	

1. Preheat the air fryer to 200ºC. 2. Air fry the bacon for 6 to 10 minutes until crispy, shaking the basket a few times while it cooks to help it cook evenly. Remove the bacon and set it aside on a paper towel. 3. Air fry the brioche bread cubes for 2 minutes to dry and toast lightly. (If your brioche is a few days old and slightly stale, you can omit this step.) 4. Butter a cake pan. Combine all the ingredients in a large bowl and toss well. Transfer the mixture to the buttered cake pan, cover with aluminum foil and refrigerate the bread pudding overnight, or for at least 8 hours. 5. Remove the casserole from the refrigerator an hour before you plan to cook, and let it sit on the countertop to come to room temperature. 6. Preheat the air fryer to 170ºC. Transfer the covered cake pan, to the basket of the air fryer, lowering the dish into the basket using a sling made of aluminum foil (fold a piece of aluminum foil into a strip about 2-inches wide by 24-inches long). Fold the ends of the aluminum foil over the top of the dish before returning the basket to the air fryer. Air fry for 20 minutes. Remove the foil and air fry for an additional 20 minutes. If the top starts to brown a little too much before the custard has set, simply return the foil to the pan. The bread pudding has cooked through when a skewer inserted into the center comes out clean.

Broccoli-Mushroom Frittata

Prep time: 10 minutes | Cook time: 20 minutes | Serves 2

1 tablespoon rapeseed oil	½ teaspoon salt
350 g broccoli florets, finely chopped	¼ teaspoon freshly ground black pepper
120 g sliced brown mushrooms	6 eggs
60 g finely chopped onion	60 g Parmesan cheese

1. In a nonstick cake pan, combine the rapeseed oil, broccoli, mushrooms, onion, salt, and pepper. Stir until the vegetables are thoroughly coated with oil. Place the cake pan in the air fryer basket and set the air fryer to 200ºC. Air fry for 5 minutes until the vegetables soften. 2. Meanwhile, in a medium bowl, whisk the eggs and Parmesan until thoroughly combined. Pour the egg mixture into the pan and shake gently to distribute the vegetables. Air fry for another 15 minutes until the eggs are set. 3. Remove from the air fryer and let sit for 5 minutes to cool slightly. Use a silicone spatula to gently lift the frittata onto a plate before serving.

Easy Sausage Pizza

Prep time: 10 minutes | Cook time: 6 minutes | Serves 4

2 tablespoons ketchup	230 g Cheddar cheese
1 pitta bread	1 teaspoon garlic powder
80 g sausage meat	1 tablespoon rapeseed oil

1. Preheat the air fryer to 170ºC. 2. Spread the ketchup over the pitta bread. 3. Top with the sausage meat and cheese. Sprinkle with the garlic powder and rapeseed oil. 4. Put the pizza in the air fryer basket and bake for 6 minutes. 5. Serve warm.

Pancake for Two

Prep time: 5 minutes | Cook time: 30 minutes | Serves 2

120 g blanched finely ground almond flour	1 large egg
2 tablespoons granular erythritol	80 ml unsweetened almond milk
1 tablespoon salted butter, melted	½ teaspoon vanilla extract

1. In a large bowl, mix all ingredients together, then pour half the batter into an ungreased round nonstick baking dish.
2. Place dish into air fryer basket. Adjust the temperature to 160ºC and bake for 15 minutes. The pancake will be golden brown on top and firm, and a toothpick inserted in the center will come out clean when done. Repeat with remaining batter.
3. Slice in half in dish and serve warm.

Chapter 2
Family Favorites

Fish and Vegetable Tacos

Prep time: 15 minutes | Cook time: 9 to 12 minutes | Serves 4

450 g white fish fillets, such as sole or cod	cabbage
	1 large carrot, grated
2 teaspoons olive oil	120 ml low-salt salsa
3 tablespoons freshly squeezed lemon juice, divided	80 ml low-fat Greek yoghurt
	4 soft low-salt wholemeal tortillas
350 g chopped red	

1. Brush the fish with the olive oil and sprinkle with 1 tablespoon of lemon juice. 2. Air fry in the air fryer basket at 200ºC for 9 to 12 minutes, or until the fish just flakes when tested with a fork. 3. Meanwhile, in a medium bowl, stir together the remaining 2 tablespoons of lemon juice, the red cabbage, carrot, salsa, and yoghurt. 4. When the fish is cooked, remove it from the air fryer basket and break it up into large pieces. 5. Offer the fish, tortillas, and the cabbage mixture, and let each person assemble a taco.

Berry Cheesecake

Prep time: 5 minutes | Cook time: 10 minutes | Serves 4

Oil, for spraying	1 large egg
227 g soft white cheese	½ teaspoon vanilla extract
6 tablespoons sugar	¼ teaspoon lemon juice
1 tablespoon sour cream	120 g fresh mixed berries

1. Preheat the air fryer to 180ºC. 2. Line the air fryer basket with parchment and spray lightly with oil. 3. In a blender, combine the soft white cheese, sugar, sour cream, egg, vanilla, and lemon juice and blend until smooth. 4. Pour the mixture into a 4-inch springform pan. 5. Place the pan in the prepared basket. Cook for 8 to 10 minutes, or until only the very centre jiggles slightly when the pan is moved. 6. Refrigerate the cheesecake in the pan for at least 2 hours. 7. Release the sides from the springform pan, top the cheesecake with the mixed berries, and serve.

Avocado and Egg Burrito

Prep time: 10 minutes | Cook time: 3 to 5 minutes | Serves 4

2 hard-boiled egg whites, chopped	salsa, plus additional for serving (optional)
1 hard-boiled egg, chopped	1 (34 g) slice low-salt, low-fat processed cheese, torn into pieces
1 avocado, peeled, pitted, and chopped	
1 red pepper, chopped	4 low-salt wholemeal flour wraps
3 tablespoons low-salt	

1. In a medium bowl, thoroughly mix the egg whites, egg, avocado, red pepper, salsa, and cheese. 2. Place the tortillas on a work surface and evenly divide the filling among them. 3. Fold in the edges and roll up. Secure the burritos with toothpicks if necessary. 4. Put the burritos in the air fryer basket. 5. Air fry at 200ºC for 3 to 5 minutes, or until the burritos are light golden brown and crisp. 6. Serve with more salsa (if using).

Veggie Tuna Melts

Prep time: 15 minutes | Cook time: 7 to 11 minutes | Serves 4

2 low-salt wholemeal English muffins, split	and green parts, sliced
	80 ml fat-free Greek yoghurt
1 (170 g) can chunk light low-salt tuna, drained	
235 g shredded carrot	2 tablespoons low-salt wholegrain mustard
80 g chopped mushrooms	2 slices low-salt low-fat Swiss cheese, halved
2 spring onions, white	

1. Place the English muffin halves in the air fryer basket. 2. Air fry at 170ºC for 3 to 4 minutes, or until crisp. Remove from the basket and set aside. 3. In a medium bowl, thoroughly mix the tuna, carrot, mushrooms, spring onions, yoghurt, and mustard. 4. Top each half of the muffins with one-fourth of the tuna mixture and a half slice of Swiss cheese. 5. Air fry for 4 to 7 minutes, or until the tuna mixture is hot and the cheese melts and starts to brown. 6. Serve immediately.

Meatball Subs

Prep time: 15 minutes | Cook time: 19 minutes | Serves 6

Oil, for spraying	garlic
450 g 15% fat minced beef	1 large egg
120 ml Italian breadcrumbs (mixed breadcrumbs, Italian seasoning and salt)	1 teaspoon salt
	1 teaspoon freshly ground black pepper
	6 sub rolls
1 tablespoon dried minced onion	1 (510 g) jar marinara sauce
1 tablespoon minced	350 ml shredded Mozzarella cheese

Oil, for spraying 450 g 15% fat minced beef 120 ml Italian breadcrumbs (mixed breadcrumbs, Italian seasoning and salt) 1 tablespoon dried minced onion 1 tablespoon minced garlic 1 large egg 1 teaspoon salt 1 teaspoon freshly ground black pepper 6 sub rolls 1 (510 g) jar marinara sauce 350 ml shredded Mozzarella cheese

Meringue Cookies

Prep time: 15 minutes | Cook time: 1 hour 30 minutes | Makes 20 cookies

Oil, for spraying	185 g sugar
4 large egg whites	Pinch cream of tartar

1. Preheat the air fryer to 60ºC. 2.Line the air fryer basket with parchment and spray lightly with oil. 3.In a small heatproof bowl, whisk together the egg whites and sugar. 4.Fill a small saucepan halfway with water, place it over medium heat, and bring to a light simmer. 5.Place the bowl with the egg whites on the saucepan, making sure the bottom of the bowl does not touch the water. 6.Whisk the mixture until the sugar is dissolved. Transfer the mixture to a large bowl and add the cream of tartar. 7.Using an electric mixer, beat the mixture on high until it is glossy and stiff peaks form. 8.Transfer the mixture to a piping bag or a zip-top plastic bag with a corner cut off. Pipe rounds into the prepared basket. 9.You may need to work in batches, depending on the size of your air fryer. Cook for 1 hour 30 minutes. 10.Turn off the air fryer and let the meringues cool completely inside. 11.The residual heat will continue to dry them out.

Churro Bites

Prep time: 5 minutes | Cook time: 6 minutes | Makes 36 bites

Oil, for spraying	1 tablespoon ground cinnamon
1 (500 g) package frozen puffed pastry, thawed	90 g icing sugar
180 g caster sugar	1 tablespoon milk

1. Preheat the air fryer to 200ºC. 2.Line the air fryer basket with parchment and spray lightly with oil. 3.Unfold the puff pastry onto a clean work surface. Using a sharp knife, cut the dough into 36 bite-size pieces. 4.Place the dough pieces in one layer in the prepared basket, taking care not to let the pieces touch or overlap. 5.Cook for 3 minutes, flip, and cook for another 3 minutes, or until puffed and golden. In a small bowl, mix together the caster sugar and cinnamon. 6.In another small bowl, whisk together the icing sugar and milk. 7.Dredge the bites in the cinnamon-sugar mixture until evenly coated. 8.Serve with the icing on the side for dipping.

Beef Jerky

Prep time: 30 minutes | Cook time: 2 hours | Serves 8

Oil, for spraying	light muscovado sugar
450 g silverside, cut into thin, short slices	1 tablespoon minced garlic
60 ml soy sauce	1 teaspoon ground ginger
3 tablespoons packed	1 tablespoon water

1. Line the air fryer basket with parchment and spray lightly with oil. 2.Place the steak, soy sauce, brown sugar, garlic, ginger, and water in a zip-top plastic bag, seal, and shake well until evenly coated. 3.Refrigerate for 30 minutes. Place the steak in the prepared basket in a single layer. 4.You may need to work in batches, depending on the size of your air fryer. 5.Air fry at 80ºC for at least 2 hours. 6.Add more time if you like your jerky a bit tougher.

Pecan Rolls

Prep time: 20 minutes | Cook time: 20 to 24 minutes | Makes 12 rolls

220 g plain flour, plus more for dusting	40 g packed light muscovado sugar
2 tablespoons caster sugar, plus 60 ml, divided	120g chopped pecans, toasted
1 teaspoon salt	1 to 2 tablespoons oil
3 tablespoons butter, at room temperature	35g icing sugar (optional)
180 ml milk, whole or semi-skimmed	

1. In a large bowl, whisk the flour, 2 tablespoons caster sugar, and salt until blended. 2.Stir in the butter and milk briefly until a sticky dough form. In a small bowl, stir together the brown sugar and remaining 60 g caster sugar. 3.Place a piece of parchment paper on a work surface and dust it with flour. Roll the dough on the prepared surface to ¼ inch thickness. 4.Spread the sugar mixture over the dough. Sprinkle the pecans on top. Roll up the dough jelly roll-style, pinching the ends to seal. 5.Cut the dough into 12 rolls. Preheat the air fryer to 160°C. 6.Line the air fryer basket with parchment paper and spritz the parchment with oil. Place 6 rolls on the prepared parchment. Bake for 5 minutes. 7.Flip the rolls and bake for 5 to 7 minutes more until lightly browned. Repeat with the remaining rolls. 8.Sprinkle with icing sugar (if using).

Chinese-Inspired Spareribs

Prep time: 30 minutes | Cook time: 8 minutes | Serves 4

Oil, for spraying	60 ml honey
340 g pork ribs, cut into 3-inch-long pieces	2 tablespoons minced garlic
235 ml soy sauce	1 teaspoon ground ginger
140 g sugar	2 drops red food dye (optional)
120 g beef broth	

1. Line the air fryer basket with parchment and spray lightly with oil. 2.Combine the ribs, soy sauce, sugar, beef broth, honey, garlic, ginger, and food colouring (if using) in a large zip-top plastic bag, seal, and shake well until completely coated. 3.Refrigerate for at least 30 minutes. 4.Place the ribs in the prepared basket. 5.Air fry at 190°C for 8 minutes, or until the internal temperature reaches 74°C.

Chapter 3

Fast and Easy Everyday Favourites

Cheesy Potato Patties

Prep time: 5 minutes | Cook time: 10 minutes | Serves 8

900 g white potatoes	1 tablespoon fine sea salt
120 g finely chopped spring onions	½ teaspoon hot paprika
½ teaspoon freshly ground black pepper, or more to taste	475 g shredded Colby or Monterey Jack cheese
	60 ml rapeseed oil
	235 g crushed crackers

1. Preheat the air fryer to 180ºC. Boil the potatoes until soft. 2. Dry them off and peel them before mashing thoroughly, leaving no lumps. 3. Combine the mashed potatoes with spring onions, pepper, salt, paprika, and cheese. 4. Mould the mixture into balls with your hands and press with your palm to flatten them into patties. 5. In a shallow dish, combine the rapeseed oil and crushed crackers. 6. Coat the patties in the crumb mixture. 7. Bake the patties for about 10 minutes, in multiple batches if necessary. 8. Serve hot.

Cheesy Jalapeño Cornbread

Prep time: 10 minutes | Cook time: 20 minutes | Serves 8

160 ml cornmeal	sugar
80 ml plain flour	180 ml whole milk
¾ teaspoon baking powder	1 large egg, beaten
2 tablespoons margarine, melted	1 jalapeño pepper, thinly sliced
½ teaspoon rock salt	80 ml shredded extra mature Cheddar cheese
1 tablespoon granulated	Cooking spray

1. Preheat the air fryer to 152ºC. Spritz the air fryer basket with cooking spray. 2. Combine all the ingredients in a large bowl. Stir to mix well. Pour the mixture in a baking pan. 3. Arrange the pan in the preheated air fryer. Bake for 20 minutes or until a toothpick inserted in the centre of the bread comes out clean. 4. When the cooking is complete, remove the baking pan from the air fryer and allow the bread to cool for a few minutes before slicing to serve.

Beery and Crunchy Onion Rings

Prep time: 10 minutes | Cook time: 16 minutes | Serves 2 to 4

80 g plain flour	180 ml beer
1 teaspoon paprika	175 g breadcrumbs
½ teaspoon bicarbonate of soda	1 tablespoons olive oil
1 teaspoon salt	1 large Vidalia or sweet onion, peeled and sliced into ½-inch rings
½ teaspoon freshly ground black pepper	Cooking spray
1 egg, beaten	

Preheat the air fryer to 180ºC. Spritz the air fryer basket with cooking spray. Combine the flour, paprika, bicarbonate of soda, salt, and ground black pepper in a bowl. Stir to mix well. Combine the egg and beer in a separate bowl. Stir to mix well. Make a well in the centre of the flour mixture, then pour the egg mixture in the well. Stir to mix everything well. Pour the breadcrumbs and olive oil in a shallow plate. Stir to mix well. Dredge the onion rings gently into the flour and egg mixture, then shake the excess off and put into the plate of breadcrumbs. Flip to coat both sides well. Arrange the onion rings in the preheated air fryer. Air fry in batches for 16 minutes or until golden brown and crunchy. Flip the rings and put the bottom rings to the top halfway through. Serve immediately.

Simple Pea Delight

Prep time: 5 minutes | Cook time: 15 minutes | Serves 2 to 4

120 g flour	3 tablespoons pea protein
1 teaspoon baking powder	120 g chicken or turkey strips
3 eggs	
235 ml coconut milk	Pinch of sea salt
235 g soft white cheese	235 g Mozzarella cheese

1. Preheat the air fryer to 200ºC. 2. In a large bowl, mix all ingredients together using a large wooden spoon. 3. Spoon equal amounts of the mixture into muffin cups and bake for 15 minutes. 4. Serve immediately.

Traditional Queso Fundido

Prep time: 10 minutes | Cook time: 25 minutes | Serves 4

110 g fresh Mexican (or Spanish if unavailable) chorizo, casings removed	2 teaspoons ground cumin
	475 g shredded Oaxaca or Mozzarella cheese
1 medium onion, chopped	120 ml half-and-half (60 g whole milk and 60 ml cream combined)
3 cloves garlic, minced	
235 g chopped tomato	
2 jalapeños, deseeded and diced	Celery sticks or tortilla chips, for serving

1. Preheat the air fryer to 200ºC. 2. In a baking tray, combine the chorizo, onion, garlic, tomato, jalapeños, and cumin. Stir to combine. 3. Place the pan in the air fryer basket. 4. Air fry for 15 minutes, or until the sausage is cooked, stirring halfway through the cooking time to break up the sausage. 5. Add the cheese and half-and-half; stir to combine. 6. Air fry for 10 minutes, or until the cheese has melted. 7. Serve with celery sticks or tortilla chips.

Crunchy Fried Okra

Prep time: 5 minutes | Cook time: 8 to 10 minutes | Serves 4

120 g self-raising yellow cornmeal (alternatively add 1 tablespoon baking powder to cornmeal)	1 teaspoon salt
	½ teaspoon freshly ground black pepper
	2 large eggs, beaten
1 teaspoon Italian-style seasoning	475 g okra slices
	Cooking spray
1 teaspoon paprika	

1. Preheat the air fryer to 200ºC. 2. Line the air fryer basket with parchment paper. In a shallow bowl, whisk the cornmeal, Italian-style seasoning, paprika, salt, and pepper until blended. 3. Place the beaten eggs in a second shallow bowl. Add the okra to the beaten egg and stir to coat. 4. Add the egg and okra mixture to the cornmeal mixture and stir until coated. 5. Place the okra on the parchment and spritz it with oil. 6. Air fry for 4 minutes. Shake the basket, spritz the okra with oil, and air fry for 4 to 6 minutes more until lightly browned and crispy. 7. Serve immediately.

Buttery Sweet Potatoes

Prep time: 5 minutes | Cook time: 10 minutes | Serves 4

2 tablespoons melted butter	2 sweet potatoes, peeled and cut into ½-inch cubes
1 tablespoon light brown sugar	Cooking spray

1. Preheat the air fryer to 200ºC. 2. Line the air fryer basket with parchment paper. In a medium bowl, stir together the melted butter and brown sugar until blended. 3. Toss the sweet potatoes in the butter mixture until coated. Place the sweet potatoes on the parchment and spritz with oil. 4. Air fry for 5 minutes. Shake the basket, spritz the sweet potatoes with oil, and air fry for 5 minutes more until they're soft enough to cut with a fork. 5. Serve immediately.

Bacon Pinwheels

Prep time: 10 minutes | Cook time: 10 minutes | Makes 8 pinwheels

1 sheet puff pastry	8 slices bacon
2 tablespoons maple syrup	Ground black pepper, to taste
48 g brown sugar	Cooking spray

Preheat the air fryer to 180ºC. Spritz the air fryer basket with cooking spray. Roll the puff pastry into a 10-inch square with a rolling pin on a clean work surface, then cut the pastry into 8 strips. Brush the strips with maple syrup and sprinkle with sugar, leaving a 1-inch far end uncovered. Arrange each slice of bacon on each strip, leaving a ⅛-inch length of bacon hang over the end close to you. Sprinkle with black pepper. From the end close to you, roll the strips into pinwheels, then dab the uncovered end with water and seal the rolls. Arrange the pinwheels in the preheated air fryer and spritz with cooking spray. Air fry for 10 minutes or until golden brown. Flip the pinwheels halfway through. Serve immediately.

Air Fried Butternut Squash with Chopped Hazelnuts

Prep time: 10 minutes | Cook time: 20 minutes | Makes 700 ml

2 tablespoons whole hazelnuts	¼ teaspoon rock salt
700 g butternut squash, peeled, deseeded, and cubed	¼ teaspoon freshly ground black pepper
	2 teaspoons olive oil
	Cooking spray

1. Preheat the air fryer to 150ºC. 2.Spritz the air fryer basket with cooking spray. 3.Arrange the hazelnuts in the preheated air fryer. Air fry for 3 minutes or until soft. 4.Chopped the hazelnuts roughly and transfer to a small bowl. Set aside. 5.Set the air fryer temperature to 180ºC. 6.Spritz with cooking spray. Put the butternut squash in a large bowl, then sprinkle with salt and pepper and drizzle with olive oil. 7.Toss to coat well. Transfer the squash in the air fryer. Air fry for 20 minutes or until the squash is soft. 8.Shake the basket halfway through the frying time. 9.When the frying is complete, transfer the squash onto a plate and sprinkle with chopped hazelnuts before serving.

Beetroot Salad with Lemon Vinaigrette

Prep time: 10 minutes | Cook time: 12 to 15 minutes | Serves 4

6 medium red and golden beetroots, peeled and sliced	2 kg mixed greens
	Cooking spray
1 teaspoon olive oil	Vinaigrette:
¼ teaspoon rock salt	2 teaspoons olive oil
120 g crumbled feta cheese	2 tablespoons chopped fresh chives
	Juice of 1 lemon

1. Preheat the air fryer to 180ºC. 2.In a large bowl, toss the beetroots, olive oil, and rock salt. 3.Spray the air fryer basket with cooking spray, then place the beetroots in the basket and air fry for 12 to 15 minutes or until tender. 4.While the beetroots cook, make the vinaigrette in a large bowl by whisking together the olive oil, lemon juice, and chives. 5.Remove the beetroots from the air fryer, toss in the vinaigrette, and allow to cool for 5 minutes. 6.Add the feta and serve on top of the mixed greens.

Sweet Corn and Carrot Fritters

Prep time: 10 minutes | Cook time: 8 to 11 minutes | Serves 4

1 medium-sized carrot, grated	1 medium-sized egg, whisked
1 yellow onion, finely chopped	2 tablespoons plain milk
4 ounces (113 g) canned sweet corn kernels, drained	1 cup grated Parmesan cheese
	¼ cup flour
1 teaspoon sea salt flakes	⅓ teaspoon baking powder
1 tablespoon chopped fresh cilantro	⅓ teaspoon sugar
	Cooking spray

1. Preheat the air fryer to 350ºF (177ºC). 2. Place the grated carrot in a colander and press down to squeeze out any excess moisture. Dry it with a paper towel. 3. Combine the carrots with the remaining ingredients. 4. Mold 1 tablespoon of the mixture into a ball and press it down with your hand or a spoon to flatten it. Repeat until the rest of the mixture is used up. 5. Spritz the balls with cooking spray. 6. Arrange in the air fryer basket, taking care not to overlap any balls. Bake for 8 to 11 minutes, or until they're firm. 7. Serve warm.

Simple and Easy Croutons

Prep time: 5 minutes | Cook time: 8 minutes | Serves 4

2 sliced bread	Hot soup, for serving
1 tablespoon olive oil	

1. Preheat the air fryer to 200ºC. 2.Cut the slices of bread into medium-size chunks. 3.Brush the air fryer basket with the oil. 4.Place the chunks inside and air fry for at least 8 minutes. 5.Serve with hot soup.

Easy Roasted Asparagus

Prep time: 5 minutes | Cook time: 6 minutes | Serves 4

450 g asparagus, trimmed and halved crosswise	Salt and pepper, to taste
1 teaspoon extra-virgin olive oil	Lemon wedges, for serving

1. Preheat the air fryer to 200ºC. 2. Toss the asparagus with the oil, ⅛ teaspoon salt, and ⅛ teaspoon pepper in bowl. Transfer to air fryer basket. 3. Place the basket in air fryer and roast for 6 to 8 minutes, or until tender and bright green, tossing halfway through cooking. 4. Season with salt and pepper and serve with lemon wedges.

Corn Fritters

Prep time: 15 minutes | Cook time: 8 minutes | Serves 6

120 g self-raising flour	60 g buttermilk
1 tablespoon sugar	180 g corn kernels
1 teaspoon salt	60 g minced onion
1 large egg, lightly beaten	Cooking spray

1. Preheat the air fryer to 180ºC. 2. Line the air fryer basket with parchment paper. In a medium bowl, whisk the flour, sugar, and salt until blended. Stir in the egg and buttermilk. 3. Add the corn and minced onion. 4. Mix well. Shape the corn fritter batter into 12 balls. 5. Place the fritters on the parchment and spritz with oil. Bake for 4 minutes. 6. Flip the fritters, spritz them with oil, and bake for 4 minutes more until firm and lightly browned. 7. Serve immediately.

Scalloped Veggie Mix

Prep time: 10 minutes | Cook time: 15 minutes | Serves 4

1 Yukon Gold or other small white potato, thinly sliced	3 garlic cloves, minced
1 small sweet potato, peeled and thinly sliced	180 ml 2 percent milk
1 medium carrot, thinly sliced	2 tablespoons cornflour
60 g minced onion	½ teaspoon dried thyme

1. Preheat the air fryer to 190ºC. 2. In a baking tray, layer the potato, sweet potato, carrot, onion, and garlic. 3. In a small bowl, whisk the milk, cornflour, and thyme until blended. 4. Pour the milk mixture evenly over the vegetables in the pan. Bake for 15 minutes. 5. Check the casserole—it should be golden brown on top, and the vegetables should be tender. 6. Serve immediately.

Chapter 4

Poultry

Pork Rind Fried Chicken

Prep time: 30 minutes | Cook time: 20 minutes | Serves 4

60 ml buffalo sauce	¼ teaspoon ground black pepper
4 (115 g) boneless, skinless chicken breasts	60 g g plain pork rinds, finely crushed
½ teaspoon paprika	
½ teaspoon garlic powder	

1. Pour buffalo sauce into a large sealable bowl or bag. Add chicken and toss to coat. Place sealed bowl or bag into refrigerator and let marinate at least 30 minutes up to overnight. 2. Remove chicken from marinade but do not shake excess sauce off chicken. Sprinkle both sides of thighs with paprika, garlic powder, and pepper. 3. Place pork rinds into a large bowl and press each chicken breast into pork rinds to coat evenly on both sides. 4. Place chicken into ungreased air fryer basket. Adjust the temperature to 200ºC and roast for 20 minutes, turning chicken halfway through cooking. Chicken will be golden and have an internal temperature of at least 76ºC when done. Serve warm.

Bruschetta Chicken

Prep time: 10 minutes | Cook time: 20 minutes | Serves 4

Bruschetta Stuffing:

1 tomato, diced	2 tablespoons chopped fresh basil
3 tablespoons balsamic vinegar	3 garlic cloves, minced
1 teaspoon Italian seasoning	2 tablespoons extra-virgin olive oil

Chicken:

4 (115 g) boneless, skinless chicken breasts, cut 4 slits each	seasoning
	Chicken seasoning or rub, to taste
1 teaspoon Italian	Cooking spray

1. Preheat the air fryer to 190º. Spritz the air fryer basket with cooking spray. 2. Combine the ingredients for the bruschetta stuffing in a bowl. Stir to mix well. Set aside. 3. Rub the chicken breasts with Italian seasoning and chicken seasoning on a clean work surface. 4. Arrange the chicken breasts, slits side up, in a single layer in the air fryer basket and spritz with cooking spray. You may need to work in batches to avoid overcrowding. 5. Air fry for 7 minutes, then open the air fryer and fill the slits in the chicken with the bruschetta stuffing. Cook for another 3 minutes or until the chicken is well browned. 6. Serve immediately.

Crunchy Chicken with Roasted Carrots

Prep time: 10 minutes | Cook time: 22 minutes | Serves 4

4 bone-in, skin-on chicken thighs	1 teaspoon sea salt, divided
2 carrots, cut into 2-inch pieces	2 teaspoons chopped fresh rosemary leaves
2 tablespoons extra-virgin olive oil	Cooking oil spray
2 teaspoons poultry spice	500 g cooked white rice

1. Brush the chicken thighs and carrots with olive oil. Sprinkle both with the poultry spice, salt, and rosemary. 2. Insert the crisper plate into the basket and the basket into the unit. Preheat the unit by selecting AIR FRY, setting the temperature to 200ºC, and setting the time to 3 minutes. Select START/STOP to begin. 3. Once the unit is preheated, spray the crisper plate with cooking oil. Place the carrots into the basket. Add the wire rack and arrange the chicken thighs on the rack. 4. Select AIR FRY, set the temperature to 200ºC, and set the time to 20 minutes. Select START/STOP to begin. 5. When the cooking is complete, check the chicken temperature. If a food thermometer inserted into the chicken registers 76ºC, remove the chicken from the air fryer, place it on a clean plate, and cover with aluminum foil to keep warm. Otherwise, resume cooking for 1 to 2 minutes longer. 6. The carrots can cook for 18 to 22 minutes and will be tender and caramelized; cooking time isn't as crucial for root vegetables. 7. Serve the chicken and carrots with the hot cooked rice.

Personal Cauliflower Pizzas

Prep time: 10 minutes | Cook time: 25 minutes | Serves 2

1 (340 g) bag frozen riced cauliflower	added marinara sauce, divided
75 g shredded Mozzarella cheese	110 g fresh Mozzarella, chopped, divided
15 g almond flour	140 g cooked chicken breast, chopped, divided
20 g Parmesan cheese	100 g chopped cherry tomatoes, divided
1 large egg	
½ teaspoon salt	
1 teaspoon garlic powder	5 g fresh baby rocket, divided
1 teaspoon dried oregano	
4 tablespoons no-sugar-	

1. Preheat the air fryer to 200°C. Cut 4 sheets of parchment paper to fit the basket of the air fryer. Brush with olive oil and set aside. 2. In a large glass bowl, microwave the cauliflower according to package directions. Place the cauliflower on a clean towel, draw up the sides, and squeeze tightly over a sink to remove the excess moisture. Return the cauliflower to the bowl and add the shredded Mozzarella along with the almond flour, Parmesan, egg, salt, garlic powder, and oregano. Stir until thoroughly combined. 3. Divide the dough into two equal portions. Place one piece of dough on the prepared parchment paper and pat gently into a thin, flat disk 7 to 8 inches in diameter. Air fry for 15 minutes until the crust begins to brown. Let cool for 5 minutes. 4. Transfer the parchment paper with the crust on top to a baking sheet. Place a second sheet of parchment paper over the crust. While holding the edges of both sheets together, carefully lift the crust off the baking sheet, flip it, and place it back in the air fryer basket. The new sheet of parchment paper is now on the bottom. Remove the top piece of paper and air fry the crust for another 15 minutes until the top begins to brown. Remove the basket from the air fryer. 5. Spread 2 tablespoons of the marinara sauce on top of the crust, followed by half the fresh Mozzarella, chicken, cherry tomatoes, and rocket. Air fry for 5 to 10 minutes longer, until the cheese is melted and beginning to brown. Remove the pizza from the oven and let it sit for 10 minutes before serving. Repeat with the remaining ingredients to make a second pizza.

Italian Chicken Thighs

Prep time: 5 minutes | Cook time: 20 minutes | Serves 2

4 bone-in, skin-on chicken thighs	1 teaspoon dried basil
2 tablespoons unsalted butter, melted	½ teaspoon garlic powder
	¼ teaspoon onion powder
	¼ teaspoon dried oregano
1 teaspoon dried parsley	

1. Brush chicken thighs with butter and sprinkle remaining ingredients over thighs. Place thighs into the air fryer basket. 2. Adjust the temperature to 190°C and roast for 20 minutes. 3. Halfway through the cooking time, flip the thighs. 4. When fully cooked, internal temperature will be at least 76°C and skin will be crispy. Serve warm.

Crunchy Chicken Tenders

Prep time: 5 minutes | Cook time: 12 minutes | Serves 4

1 egg	½ teaspoon black pepper
60 ml unsweetened almond milk	½ teaspoon dried thyme
	½ teaspoon dried sage
15 g whole wheat flour	½ teaspoon garlic powder
15 g whole wheat bread crumbs	450 g chicken tenderloins
	1 lemon, quartered
½ teaspoon salt	

1. Preheat the air fryer to 184°C. 2. In a shallow bowl, beat together the egg and almond milk until frothy. 3. In a separate shallow bowl, whisk together the flour, bread crumbs, salt, pepper, thyme, sage, and garlic powder. 4. Dip each chicken tenderloin into the egg mixture, then into the bread crumb mixture, coating the outside with the crumbs. Place the breaded chicken tenderloins into the bottom of the air fryer basket in an even layer, making sure that they don't touch each other. 5. Cook for 6 minutes, then turn and cook for an additional 5 to 6 minutes. Serve with lemon slices.

Almond-Crusted Chicken

Prep time: 15 minutes | Cook time: 25 minutes | Serves 4

20 g slivered almonds	mayonnaise
2 (170 g) boneless, skinless chicken breasts	1 tablespoon Dijon mustard
2 tablespoons full-fat	

1. Pulse the almonds in a food processor or chop until finely chopped. Place almonds evenly on a plate and set aside. 2. Completely slice each chicken breast in half lengthwise. 3. Mix the mayonnaise and mustard in a small bowl and then coat chicken with the mixture. 4. Lay each piece of chicken in the chopped almonds to fully coat. Carefully move the pieces into the air fryer basket. 5. Adjust the temperature to 180°C and air fry for 25 minutes. 6. Chicken will be done when it has reached an internal temperature of 76°C or more. Serve warm.

Teriyaki Chicken Thighs with Lemony Snow Peas

Prep time: 30 minutes | Cook time: 34 minutes | Serves 4

60 ml chicken broth	1 tablespoon sugar
½ teaspoon grated fresh ginger	170 g mangetout, strings removed
⅛ teaspoon red pepper flakes	⅛ teaspoon lemon zest
	1 garlic clove, minced
1½ tablespoons soy sauce	¼ teaspoon salt
4 (140 g) bone-in chicken thighs, trimmed	Ground black pepper, to taste
1 tablespoon mirin	½ teaspoon lemon juice
½ teaspoon cornflour	

1. Combine the broth, ginger, pepper flakes, and soy sauce in a large bowl. Stir to mix well. 2. Pierce 10 to 15 holes into the chicken skin. Put the chicken in the broth mixture and toss to coat well. Let sit for 10 minutes to marinate. 3. Preheat the air fryer to 206°C. 4. Transfer the marinated chicken on a plate and pat dry with paper towels. 5. Scoop 2 tablespoons of marinade in a microwave-safe bowl and combine with mirin, cornflour and sugar. Stir to mix well. Microwave for 1 minute or until frothy and has a thick consistency. Set aside. 6. Arrange the chicken in the preheated air fryer, skin side up, and air fry for 25 minutes or until the internal temperature of the chicken reaches at least 76°C. Gently turn the chicken over halfway through. 7. When the frying is complete, brush the chicken skin with marinade mixture. Air fryer the chicken for 5 more minutes or until glazed. 8. Remove the chicken from the air fryer and reserve ½ teaspoon of chicken fat remains in the air fryer. Allow the chicken to cool for 10 minutes. 9. Meanwhile, combine the reserved chicken fat, snow peas, lemon zest, garlic, salt, and ground black pepper in a small bowl. Toss to coat well. 10. Transfer the snow peas in the air fryer and air fry for 3 minutes or until soft. Remove the peas from the air fryer and toss with lemon juice. 11. Serve the chicken with lemony snow peas.

Spanish Chicken and Mini Sweet Pepper Baguette

Prep time: 10 minutes | Cook time: 20 minutes | Serves 2

570 g assorted small chicken parts, breasts cut into halves	230 g mini sweet peppers
	60 g light mayonnaise
¼ teaspoon salt	¼ teaspoon smoked paprika
¼ teaspoon ground black pepper	½ clove garlic, crushed
	Baguette, for serving
2 teaspoons olive oil	Cooking spray

1. Preheat air fryer to 190°C. Spritz the air fryer basket with cooking spray. 2. Toss the chicken with salt, ground black pepper, and olive oil in a large bowl. 3. Arrange the sweet peppers and chicken in the preheated air fryer and air fry for 10 minutes, then transfer the peppers on a plate. 4. Flip the chicken and air fry for 10 more minutes or until well browned. 5. Meanwhile, combine the mayo, paprika, and garlic in a small bowl. Stir to mix well. 6. Assemble the baguette with chicken and sweet pepper, then spread with mayo mixture and serve.

Lemon Chicken with Garlic

Prep time: 5 minutes | Cook time: 20 to 25 minutes | Serves 4

8 bone-in chicken thighs, skin on	½ teaspoon paprika
1 tablespoon olive oil	½ teaspoon garlic powder
1½ teaspoons lemon-pepper seasoning	¼ teaspoon freshly ground black pepper
	Juice of ½ lemon

1. Preheat the air fryer to 180°C. 2. Place the chicken in a large bowl and drizzle with the olive oil. Top with the lemon-pepper seasoning, paprika, garlic powder, and freshly ground black pepper. Toss until thoroughly coated. 3. Working in batches if necessary, arrange the chicken in a single layer in the basket of the air fryer. Pausing halfway through the cooking time to turn the chicken, air fry for 20 to 25 minutes, until a thermometer inserted into the thickest piece registers 76°C. 4. Transfer the chicken to a serving platter and squeeze the lemon juice over the top.

Coriander Lime Chicken Thighs

Prep time: 15 minutes | Cook time: 22 minutes | Serves 4

4 bone-in, skin-on chicken thighs	1 teaspoon cumin
1 teaspoon baking powder	2 medium limes
½ teaspoon garlic powder	5 g chopped fresh coriander
2 teaspoons chili powder	

1. Pat chicken thighs dry and sprinkle with baking powder. 2. In a small bowl, mix garlic powder, chili powder, and cumin and sprinkle evenly over thighs, gently rubbing on and under chicken skin. 3. Cut one lime in half and squeeze juice over thighs. Place chicken into the air fryer basket. 4. Adjust the temperature to 190°C and roast for 22 minutes. 5. Cut other lime into four wedges for serving and garnish cooked chicken with wedges and coriander.

Crispy Duck with Cherry Sauce

Prep time: 10 minutes | Cook time: 33 minutes | Serves 2 to 4

1 whole duck (2.3 kg), split in half, back and rib bones removed	1 teaspoon olive oil
	Salt and freshly ground black pepper, to taste

Cherry Sauce:

1 tablespoon butter	vinegar
1 shallot, minced	1 teaspoon fresh thyme leaves
120 ml sherry	
240 g cherry preserves	Salt and freshly ground black pepper, to taste
240 ml chicken stock	
1 teaspoon white wine	

1. Preheat the air fryer to 200°C. 2. Trim some of the fat from the duck. Rub olive oil on the duck and season with salt and pepper. Place the duck halves in the air fryer basket, breast side up and facing the centre of the basket. 3. Air fry the duck for 20 minutes. Turn the duck over and air fry for another 6 minutes. 4. While duck is air frying, make the cherry sauce. Melt the butter in a large sauté pan. Add the shallot and sauté until it is just starting to brown, about 2 to 3 minutes. Add the sherry and deglaze the pan by scraping up any brown bits from the bottom of the pan. Simmer the liquid for a few minutes, until it has reduced by half. Add the cherry preserves, chicken stock and white wine vinegar. Whisk well to combine all the ingredients. Simmer the sauce until it thickens and coats the back of a spoon, about 5 to 7 minutes. Season with salt and pepper and stir in the fresh thyme leaves. 5. When the air fryer timer goes off, spoon some cherry sauce over the duck and continue to air fry at 200°C for 4 more minutes. Then, turn the duck halves back over so that the breast side is facing up. Spoon more cherry sauce over the top of the duck, covering the skin completely. Air fry for 3 more minutes and then remove the duck to a plate to rest for a few minutes. 6. Serve the duck in halves, or cut each piece in half again for a smaller serving. Spoon any additional sauce over the duck or serve it on the side.

Chicken Manchurian

Prep time: 10 minutes | Cook time: 20 minutes | Serves 2

450 g boneless, skinless chicken breasts, cut into 1-inch pieces	1 teaspoon hot sauce, such as Tabasco
60 g ketchup	½ teaspoon garlic powder
1 tablespoon tomato-based chili sauce, such as Heinz	¼ teaspoon cayenne pepper
1 tablespoon soy sauce	2 spring onions, thinly sliced
1 tablespoon rice vinegar	Cooked white rice, for serving
2 teaspoons vegetable oil	

1. Preheat the air fryer to 180°C. 2. In a bowl, combine the chicken, ketchup, chili sauce, soy sauce, vinegar, oil, hot sauce, garlic powder, cayenne, and three-quarters of the spring onions and toss until evenly coated. 3. Scrape the chicken and sauce into a metal cake pan and place the pan in the air fryer. Bake until the chicken is cooked through and the sauce is reduced to a thick glaze, about 20 minutes, flipping the chicken pieces halfway through. 4. Remove the pan from the air fryer. Spoon the chicken and sauce over rice and top with the remaining spring onions. Serve immediately.

Italian Chicken with Sauce

Prep time: 15 minutes | Cook time: 20 minutes | Serves 4

2 large skinless chicken breasts (about 565 g)	seasoning
	1 egg, lightly beaten
Salt and freshly ground black pepper	1 tablespoon olive oil
25 g almond meal	225 g no-sugar-added marinara sauce
45 g grated Parmesan cheese	4 slices Mozzarella cheese or 110 g shredded Mozzarella
2 teaspoons Italian	

1. Preheat the air fryer to 180°C. 2. Slice the chicken breasts in half horizontally to create 4 thinner chicken breasts. Working with one piece at a time, place the chicken between two pieces of parchment paper and pound with a meat mallet or rolling pin to flatten to an even thickness. Season both sides with salt and freshly ground black pepper. 3. In a large shallow bowl, combine the almond meal, Parmesan, and Italian seasoning; stir until thoroughly combined. Place the egg in another large shallow bowl. 4. Dip the chicken in the egg, followed by the almond meal mixture, pressing the mixture firmly into the chicken to create an even coating. 5. Working in batches if necessary, arrange the chicken breasts in a single layer in the air fryer basket and coat both sides lightly with olive oil. Pausing halfway through the cooking time to flip the chicken, air fry for 15 minutes, or until a thermometer inserted into the thickest part registers 76°C. 6. Spoon the marinara sauce over each piece of chicken and top with the Mozzarella cheese. Air fry for an additional 3 to 5 minutes until the cheese is melted.

Jerk Chicken Thighs

Prep time: 30 minutes | Cook time: 15 to 20 minutes | Serves 6

2 teaspoons ground coriander	1 teaspoon dried thyme
1 teaspoon ground allspice	½ teaspoon ground cinnamon
1 teaspoon cayenne pepper	½ teaspoon ground nutmeg
1 teaspoon ground ginger	900 g boneless chicken thighs, skin on
1 teaspoon salt	2 tablespoons olive oil

1. In a small bowl, combine the coriander, allspice, cayenne, ginger, salt, thyme, cinnamon, and nutmeg. Stir until thoroughly combined. 2. Place the chicken in a baking dish and use paper towels to pat dry. Thoroughly coat both sides of the chicken with the spice mixture. Cover and refrigerate for at least 2 hours, preferably overnight. 3. Preheat the air fryer to 180°C. 4. Working in batches if necessary, arrange the chicken in a single layer in the air fryer basket and lightly coat with the olive oil. Pausing halfway through the cooking time to flip the chicken, air fry for 15 to 20 minutes, until a thermometer inserted into the thickest part registers 76°C.

Chicken Wings with Piri Piri Sauce

Prep time: 30 minutes | Cook time: 30 minutes | Serves 6

12 chicken wings	½ teaspoon cumin powder
45 g butter, melted	1 teaspoon garlic paste
1 teaspoon onion powder	

Sauce:

60 g piri piri peppers, stemmed and chopped	2 tablespoons fresh lemon juice
1 tablespoon pimiento, seeded and minced	⅓ teaspoon sea salt
1 garlic clove, chopped	½ teaspoon tarragon

1. Steam the chicken wings using a steamer basket that is placed over a saucepan with boiling water; reduce the heat. 2. Now, steam the wings for 10 minutes over a moderate heat. Toss the wings with butter, onion powder, cumin powder, and garlic paste. 3. Let the chicken wings cool to room temperature. Then, refrigerate them for 45 to 50 minutes. 4. Roast in the preheated air fryer at 170ºC for 25 to 30 minutes; make sure to flip them halfway through. 5. While the chicken wings are cooking, prepare the sauce by mixing all of the sauce ingredients in a food processor. Toss the wings with prepared Piri Piri Sauce and serve.

Sweet Chili Spiced Chicken

Prep time: 10 minutes | Cook time: 43 minutes | Serves 4

Spice Rub:

2 tablespoons brown sugar	salt or kosher salt
2 tablespoons paprika	2 teaspoons coarsely ground black pepper
1 teaspoon dry mustard powder	1 tablespoon vegetable oil
1 teaspoon chili powder	1 (1.6 kg) chicken, cut into 8 pieces
2 tablespoons coarse sea	

1. Prepare the spice rub by combining the brown sugar, paprika, mustard powder, chili powder, salt and pepper. Rub the oil all over the chicken pieces and then rub the spice mix onto the chicken, covering completely. This is done very easily in a zipper sealable bag. You can do this ahead of time and let the chicken marinate in the refrigerator, or just proceed with cooking right away. 2. Preheat the air fryer to 190ºC. 3. Air fry the chicken in two batches. Place the two chicken thighs and two drumsticks into the air fryer basket. Air fry at 190ºC for 10 minutes. Then, gently turn the chicken pieces over and air fry for another 10 minutes. Remove the chicken pieces and let them rest on a plate while you cook the chicken breasts. Air fry the chicken breasts, skin side down for 8 minutes. Turn the chicken breasts over and air fry for another 12 minutes. 4. Lower the temperature of the air fryer to 170ºC. Place the first batch of chicken on top of the second batch already in the basket and air fry for a final 3 minutes. 5. Let the chicken rest for 5 minutes and serve warm with some mashed potatoes and a green salad or vegetables.

Turkish Chicken Kebabs

Prep time: 30 minutes | Cook time: 15 minutes | Serves 4

70 g plain Greek yogurt	Hungarian paprika
1 tablespoon minced garlic	½ teaspoon ground cinnamon
1 tablespoon tomato paste	
1 tablespoon fresh lemon juice	½ teaspoon black pepper
1 tablespoon vegetable oil	½ teaspoon cayenne pepper
1 teaspoon kosher salt	450 g boneless, skinless chicken thighs, quartered crosswise
1 teaspoon ground cumin	
1 teaspoon sweet	

1. In a large bowl, combine the yogurt, garlic, tomato paste, lemon juice, vegetable oil, salt, cumin, paprika, cinnamon, black pepper, and cayenne. Stir until the spices are blended into the yogurt. 2. Add the chicken to the bowl and toss until well coated. Marinate at room temperature for 30 minutes, or cover and refrigerate for up to 24 hours. 3. Arrange the chicken in a single layer in the air fryer basket. Set the air fryer to (190ºC for 10 minutes. Turn the chicken and cook for 5 minutes more. Use a meat thermometer to ensure the chicken has reached an internal temperature of 76ºC.

Cranberry Curry Chicken

Prep time: 12 minutes | Cook time: 18 minutes | Serves 4

3 (140 g) low-sodium boneless, skinless chicken breasts, cut into 1½-inch cubes	1 tart apple, chopped
	120 ml low-sodium chicken broth
	60 g dried cranberries
2 teaspoons olive oil	2 tablespoons freshly squeezed orange juice
2 tablespoons cornflour	
1 tablespoon curry powder	Brown rice, cooked (optional)

1. Preheat the air fryer to 196°C. 2. In a medium bowl, mix the chicken and olive oil. Sprinkle with the cornflour and curry powder. Toss to coat. Stir in the apple and transfer to a metal pan. Bake in the air fryer for 8 minutes, stirring once during cooking. 3. Add the chicken broth, cranberries, and orange juice. Bake for about 10 minutes more, or until the sauce is slightly thickened and the chicken reaches an internal temperature of 76°C on a meat thermometer. Serve over hot cooked brown rice, if desired.

Apricot-Glazed Turkey Tenderloin

Prep time: 20 minutes | Cook time: 30 minutes | Serves 4

Olive oil	680 g turkey breast tenderloin
80 g sugar-free apricot preserves	
½ tablespoon spicy brown mustard	Salt and freshly ground black pepper, to taste

1. Spray the air fryer basket lightly with olive oil. 2. In a small bowl, combine the apricot preserves and mustard to make a paste. 3. Season the turkey with salt and pepper. Spread the apricot paste all over the turkey. 4. Place the turkey in the air fryer basket and lightly spray with olive oil. 5. Air fry at 190°C for 15 minutes. Flip the turkey over and lightly spray with olive oil. Air fry until the internal temperature reaches at least 80°C, an additional 10 to 15 minutes. 6. Let the turkey rest for 10 minutes before slicing and serving.

Lettuce-Wrapped Turkey and Mushroom Meatballs

Prep time: 10 minutes | Cook time: 15 minutes | Serves 6

Sauce:

2 tablespoons tamari	a paste
2 tablespoons tomato sauce	120 ml chicken broth
	55 g sugar
1 tablespoon lime juice	2 tablespoons toasted sesame oil
¼ teaspoon peeled and grated fresh ginger	
	Cooking spray
1 clove garlic, smashed to	

Meatballs:

900 g turkey mince	garnish
75 g finely chopped button mushrooms	2 teaspoons peeled and grated fresh ginger
2 large eggs, beaten	1 clove garlic, smashed
1½ teaspoons tamari	2 teaspoons toasted sesame oil
15 g finely chopped green onions, plus more for	2 tablespoons sugar

For Serving:

Lettuce leaves, for serving	garnish (optional)
	Toasted sesame seeds, for garnish (optional)
Sliced red chilies, for	

1. Preheat the air fryer to 180°C. Spritz a baking pan with cooking spray. 2. Combine the ingredients for the sauce in a small bowl. Stir to mix well. Set aside. 3. Combine the ingredients for the meatballs in a large bowl. Stir to mix well, then shape the mixture in twelve 1½-inch meatballs. 4. Arrange the meatballs in a single layer on the baking pan, then baste with the sauce. You may need to work in batches to avoid overcrowding. 5. Arrange the pan in the air fryer. Air fry for 15 minutes or until the meatballs are golden brown. Flip the balls halfway through the cooking time. 6. Unfold the lettuce leaves on a large serving plate, then transfer the cooked meatballs on the leaves. Spread the red chilies and sesame seeds over the balls, then serve.

Easy Chicken Fingers

Prep time: 20 minutes | Cook time: 30 minutes | Makes 12 chicken fingers

30 g all-purpose flour	into 4 strips
120 g panko breadcrumbs	Kosher salt and freshly ground black pepper, to taste
2 tablespoons rapeseed oil	
1 large egg	
3 boneless and skinless chicken breasts, each cut	Cooking spray

1. Preheat the air fryer to 180°C. Spritz the air fryer basket with cooking spray. 2. Pour the flour in a large bowl. Combine the panko and rapeseed oil on a shallow dish. Whisk the egg in a separate bowl. 3. Rub the chicken strips with salt and ground black pepper on a clean work surface, then dip the chicken in the bowl of flour. Shake the excess off and dunk the chicken strips in the bowl of whisked egg, then roll the strips over the panko to coat well. 4. Arrange 4 strips in the air fryer basket each time and air fry for 10 minutes or until crunchy and lightly browned. Flip the strips halfway through. Repeat with remaining ingredients. 5. Serve immediately.

Pecan Turkey Cutlets

Prep time: 10 minutes | Cook time: 10 to 12 minutes per batch | Serves 4

45 g panko bread crumbs	15 g cornflour
¼ teaspoon salt	1 egg, beaten
¼ teaspoon pepper	450 g turkey cutlets, ½-inch thick
¼ teaspoon mustard powder	
¼ teaspoon poultry seasoning	Salt and pepper, to taste
	Oil for misting or cooking spray
50 g pecans	

1. Place the panko crumbs, ¼ teaspoon salt, ¼ teaspoon pepper, mustard, and poultry seasoning in food processor. Process until crumbs are finely crushed. Add pecans and process in short pulses just until nuts are finely chopped. Go easy so you don't overdo it! 2. Preheat the air fryer to 180°C. 3. Place cornflour in one shallow dish and beaten egg in another. Transfer coating mixture from food processor into a third shallow dish. 4. Sprinkle turkey cutlets with salt and pepper to taste. 5. Dip cutlets in cornflour and shake off excess. Then dip in beaten egg and roll in crumbs, pressing to coat well. Spray both sides with oil or cooking spray. 6. Place 2 cutlets in air fryer basket in a single layer and cook for 10 to 12 minutes or until juices run clear. 7. Repeat step 6 to cook remaining cutlets.

Turkey Meatloaf

Prep time: 10 minutes | Cook time: 50 minutes | Serves 4

230 g sliced mushrooms	2 tablespoons almond milk
1 small onion, coarsely chopped	
2 cloves garlic	1 tablespoon dried oregano
680 g 85% lean turkey mince	1 teaspoon salt
	½ teaspoon freshly ground black pepper
2 eggs, lightly beaten	
1 tablespoon tomato paste	1 Roma tomato, thinly sliced
15 g almond meal	

1. Preheat the air fryer to 180°C. . Lightly coat a round pan with olive oil and set aside. 2. In a food processor fitted with a metal blade, combine the mushrooms, onion, and garlic. Pulse until finely chopped. Transfer the vegetables to a large mixing bowl. 3. Add the turkey, eggs, tomato paste, almond meal, milk, oregano, salt, and black pepper. Mix gently until thoroughly combined. Transfer the mixture to the prepared pan and shape into a loaf. Arrange the tomato slices on top. 4. Air fry for 50 minutes or until the meatloaf is nicely browned and a thermometer inserted into the thickest part registers 76°C. Remove from the air fryer and let rest for about 10 minutes before slicing.

Chapter 5
Beef, Pork, and Lamb

Pork Medallions with Endive Salad

Prep time: 25 minutes | Cook time: 7 minutes | Serves 4

1 (230 g) pork tenderloin	1 teaspoon mustard powder
Salt and freshly ground black pepper, to taste	1 teaspoon garlic powder
30 g flour	1 teaspoon dried thyme
2 eggs, lightly beaten	1 teaspoon salt
180 g finely crushed crackers	vegetable or rapeseed oil, in spray bottle
1 teaspoon paprika	

Vinaigrette:

60 ml white balsamic vinegar	2 tablespoons chopped chervil or flat-leaf parsley
2 tablespoons agave syrup (or honey or maple syrup)	salt and freshly ground black pepper
1 tablespoon Dijon mustard	120 ml extra-virgin olive oil
juice of ½ lemon	

Endive Salad:

1 heart romaine lettuce, torn into large pieces	85 g fresh Mozzarella, diced
2 heads endive, sliced	Salt and freshly ground black pepper, to taste
120 g cherry tomatoes, halved	

1. Slice the pork tenderloin into 1-inch slices. Using a meat pounder, pound the pork slices into thin ½-inch medallions. Generously season the pork with salt and freshly ground black pepper on both sides. 2. Set up a dredging station using three shallow dishes. Put the flour in one dish and the beaten eggs in a second dish. Combine the crushed crackers, paprika, mustard powder, garlic powder, thyme and salt in a third dish. 3. Preheat the air fryer to 200°C. 4. Dredge the pork medallions in flour first and then into the beaten egg. Let the excess egg drip off and coat both sides of the medallions with the cracker crumb mixture. Spray both sides of the coated medallions with vegetable or rapeseed oil. 5. Air fry the medallions in two batches at 200°C for 5 minutes. Once you have air-fried all the medallions, flip them all over and return the first batch of medallions back into the air fryer on top of the second batch. Air fry at 200°C for an additional 2 minutes. 6. While the medallions are cooking, make the salad and dressing. Whisk the white balsamic vinegar, agave syrup, Dijon mustard, lemon juice, chervil, salt and pepper together in a small bowl. Whisk in the olive oil slowly until combined and thickened. 7. Combine the romaine lettuce, endive, cherry tomatoes, and Mozzarella cheese in a large salad bowl. Drizzle the dressing over the vegetables and toss to combine. Season with salt and freshly ground black pepper. 8. Serve the pork medallions warm on or beside the salad.

Lemon Pork with Marjoram

Prep time: 5 minutes | Cook time: 10 minutes | Serves 4

1 (450 g) pork tenderloin, cut into ½-inch-thick slices	½ teaspoon grated lemon zest
1 tablespoon extra-virgin olive oil	½ teaspoon dried marjoram leaves
1 tablespoon freshly squeezed lemon juice	Pinch salt
1 tablespoon honey	Freshly ground black pepper, to taste
	Cooking oil spray

1. Put the pork slices in a medium bowl. 2. In a small bowl, whisk the olive oil, lemon juice, honey, lemon zest, marjoram, salt, and pepper until combined. Pour this marinade over the tenderloin slices and gently massage with your hands to work it into the pork. 3. Insert the crisper plate into the basket and the basket into the unit. Preheat the unit by selecting AIR ROAST, setting the temperature to 200°C, and setting the time to 3 minutes. Select START/STOP to begin. 4. Once the unit is preheated, spray the crisper plate with cooking oil. Place the pork into the basket. 5. Select AIR ROAST, set the temperature to 200°C, and set the time to 10 minutes. Select START/STOP to begin. 6. When the cooking is complete, a food thermometer inserted into the pork should register at least 64°C. Let the pork stand for 5 minutes and serve.

Minute Steak Roll-Ups

Prep time: 30 minutes | Cook time: 8 to 10 minutes | Serves 4

4 minute steaks (170 g each)	120 g finely chopped brown onion
1 (450 g) bottle Italian dressing	120 g finely chopped green pepper
1 teaspoon salt	120 g finely chopped mushrooms
½ teaspoon freshly ground black pepper	1 to 2 tablespoons oil

1. In a large resealable bag or airtight storage container, combine the steaks and Italian dressing. Seal the bag and refrigerate to marinate for 2 hours. 2. Remove the steaks from the marinade and place them on a cutting board. Discard the marinade. Evenly season the steaks with salt and pepper. 3. In a small bowl, stir together the onion, pepper, and mushrooms. Sprinkle the onion mixture evenly over the steaks. Roll up the steaks, jelly roll-style, and secure with toothpicks. 4. Preheat the air fryer to 200ºC. 5. Place the steaks in the air fryer basket. 6. Cook for 4 minutes. Flip the steaks and spritz them with oil. Cook for 4 to 6 minutes more until the internal temperature reaches 64ºC. Let rest for 5 minutes before serving.

Lamb Chops with Horseradish Sauce

Prep time: 30 minutes | Cook time: 13 minutes | Serves 4

Lamb:

4 lamb loin chops	½ teaspoon coarse or flaky salt
2 tablespoons vegetable oil	½ teaspoon black pepper
1 clove garlic, minced	

Horseradish Cream Sauce:

120 ml mayonnaise	grated horseradish
1 tablespoon Dijon mustard	2 teaspoons sugar
1 to 1½ tablespoons	Vegetable oil spray

1. For the lamb: Brush the lamb chops with the oil, rub with the garlic, and sprinkle with the salt and pepper. Marinate at room temperature for 30 minutes. 2. Meanwhile, for the sauce: In a medium bowl, combine the mayonnaise, mustard, horseradish, and sugar. Stir until well combined. Set aside half of the sauce for serving. 3. Spray the air fryer basket with vegetable oil spray and place the chops in the basket. Set the air fryer to 160ºC for 10 minutes, turning the chops halfway through the cooking time. 4. Remove the chops from the air fryer and add to the bowl with the horseradish sauce, turning to coat with the sauce. Place the chops back in the air fryer basket. Set the air fryer to 200ºC for 3 minutes. Use a meat thermometer to ensure the meat has reached an internal temperature of 64ºC (for medium-rare). 5. Serve the chops with the reserved horseradish sauce.

Cheese Wine Pork Loin

Prep time: 30 minutes | Cook time: 15 minutes | Serves 2

235 ml water	powder
235 ml red wine	Sea salt and ground black pepper, to taste
1 tablespoon sea salt	
2 pork loin steaks	1 egg
60 g ground almonds	60 ml yoghurt
30 g flaxseed meal	1 teaspoon wholegrain or English mustard
½ teaspoon baking powder	
1 teaspoon onion granules	80 g Parmesan cheese, grated
½ teaspoon porcini	

1. In a large ceramic dish, combine the water, wine and salt. Add the pork and put for 1 hour in the refrigerator. 2. In a shallow bowl, mix the ground almonds, flaxseed meal, baking powder, onion granules, porcini powder, salt, and ground pepper. In another bowl, whisk the eggs with yoghurt and mustard. 3. In a third bowl, place the grated Parmesan cheese. 4. Dip the pork in the seasoned flour mixture and toss evenly; then, in the egg mixture. Finally, roll them over the grated Parmesan cheese. 5. Spritz the bottom of the air fryer basket with cooking oil. Add the breaded pork and cook at 200ºC and for 10 minutes. 6. Flip and cook for 5 minutes more on the other side. Serve warm.

Kielbasa Sausage with Pineapple and Peppers

Prep time: 15 minutes | Cook time: 10 minutes | Serves 2 to 4

340 g kielbasa sausage, cut into ½-inch slices	1 tablespoon barbecue seasoning
1 (230 g) can pineapple chunks in juice, drained	1 tablespoon soy sauce
235 g pepper chunks	Cooking spray

1. Preheat the air fryer to 200°C. Spritz the air fryer basket with cooking spray. 2. Combine all the ingredients in a large bowl. Toss to mix well. 3. Pour the sausage mixture in the preheated air fryer. 4. Air fry for 10 minutes or until the sausage is lightly browned and the pepper and pineapple are soft. Shake the basket halfway through. Serve immediately.

Air Fried Beef Satay with Peanut Dipping Sauce

Prep time: 30 minutes | Cook time: 5 to 7 minutes | Serves 4

230 g bavette or skirt steak, sliced into 8 strips	½ teaspoon coarse or flaky salt
2 teaspoons curry powder	Cooking spray

Peanut Dipping sauce:

2 tablespoons creamy peanut butter	2 teaspoons rice vinegar
1 tablespoon reduced-salt soy sauce	1 teaspoon honey
	1 teaspoon grated ginger

Special Equipment:

4 bamboo skewers, cut into halves and soaked in water for 20 minutes to	keep them from burning while cooking

1. Preheat the air fryer to 180°C. Spritz the air fryer basket with cooking spray. 2. In a bowl, place the steak strips and sprinkle with the curry powder and coarse or flaky salt to season. Thread the strips onto the soaked skewers. 3. Arrange the skewers in the prepared air fryer basket and spritz with cooking spray. Air fry for 5 to 7 minutes, or until the beef is well browned, turning halfway through. 4. In the meantime, stir together the peanut butter, soy sauce, rice vinegar, honey, and ginger in a bowl to make the dipping sauce. 5. Transfer the beef to the serving dishes and let rest for 5 minutes. Serve with the peanut dipping sauce on the side.

Mexican Pork Chops

Prep time: 5 minutes | Cook time: 15 minutes | Serves 2

¼ teaspoon dried oregano	2 (110 g) boneless pork chops
1½ teaspoons taco seasoning or fajita seasoning mix	2 tablespoons unsalted butter, divided

1. Preheat the air fryer to 200°C. 2. Combine the dried oregano and taco seasoning in a small bowl and rub the mixture into the pork chops. Brush the chops with 1 tablespoon butter. 3. In the air fryer, air fry the chops for 15 minutes, turning them over halfway through to air fry on the other side. 4. When the chops are a brown color, check the internal temperature has reached 64°C and remove from the air fryer. Serve with a garnish of remaining butter.

Beef Steak Fingers

Prep time: 5 minutes | Cook time: 8 minutes | Serves 4

4 small beef minute steaks	pepper, to taste
	60 g flour
Salt and ground black	Cooking spray

1. Preheat the air fryer to 200°C. 2. Cut minute steaks into 1-inch-wide strips. 3. Sprinkle lightly with salt and pepper to taste. 4. Roll in flour to coat all sides. 5. Spritz air fryer basket with cooking spray. 6. Put steak strips in air fryer basket in a single layer. Spritz top of steak strips with cooking spray. 7. Air fry for 4 minutes, turn strips over, and spritz with cooking spray. 8. Air fry 4 more minutes and test with fork for doneness. Steak fingers should be crispy outside with no red juices inside. 9. Repeat steps 5 through 7 to air fry remaining strips. 10. Serve immediately.

Beef and Tomato Sauce Meatloaf

Prep time: 15 minutes | Cook time: 25 minutes | Serves 4

680 g beef mince	2 tablespoons minced ginger
235 ml tomato sauce	2 garlic cloves, minced
60 g breadcrumbs	½ teaspoon dried basil
2 egg whites	1 teaspoon cayenne pepper
120 g grated Parmesan cheese	Salt and ground black pepper, to taste
1 diced onion	Cooking spray
2 tablespoons chopped parsley	

1. Preheat the air fryer to 180ºC. Spritz a meatloaf pan with cooking spray. 2. Combine all the ingredients in a large bowl. Stir to mix well. 3. Pour the meat mixture in the prepared meatloaf pan and press with a spatula to make it firm. 4. Arrange the pan in the preheated air fryer and bake for 25 minutes or until the beef is well browned. 5. Serve immediately.

Bacon-Wrapped Pork Tenderloin

Prep time: 30 minutes | Cook time: 22 to 25 minutes | Serves 6

120 g minced onion	¼ teaspoon salt
120 ml apple cider, or apple juice	¼ teaspoon freshly ground black pepper
60 ml honey	900 g pork tenderloin
1 tablespoon minced garlic	1 to 2 tablespoons oil
	8 uncooked bacon slices

1. In a medium bowl, stir together the onion, cider, honey, garlic, salt, and pepper. Transfer to a large resealable bag or airtight container and add the pork. Seal the bag. Refrigerate to marinate for at least 2 hours. 2. Preheat the air fryer to 200ºC. Line the air fryer basket with parchment paper. 3. Remove the pork from the marinade and place it on the parchment. Spritz with oil. 4. Cook for 15 minutes. 5. Wrap the bacon slices around the pork and secure them with toothpicks. Turn the pork roast and spritz with oil. Cook for 7 to 10 minutes more until the internal temperature reaches 64ºC, depending on how well-done you like pork loin. It will continue cooking after it's removed from the fryer, so let it sit for 5 minutes before serving.

Steak, Broccoli, and Mushroom Rice Bowls

Prep time: 10 minutes | Cook time: 15 to 18 minutes | Serves 4

2 tablespoons cornflour	1 onion, chopped
120 ml low-sodium beef stock	235 g sliced white or chestnut mushrooms
1 teaspoon reduced-salt soy sauce	1 tablespoon grated peeled fresh ginger
340 g rump steak, cut into 1-inch cubes	Cooked brown rice (optional), for serving
120 g broccoli florets	

1. In a medium bowl, stir together the cornflour, beef stock, and soy sauce until the cornflour is completely dissolved. 2. Add the beef cubes and toss to coat. Let stand for 5 minutes at room temperature. 3. Insert the crisper plate into the basket and the basket into the unit. Preheat the unit by selecting AIR FRY, setting the temperature to 200ºC, and setting the time to 3 minutes. Select START/STOP to begin. 4. Once the unit is preheated, use a slotted spoon to transfer the beef from the stock mixture into a medium metal bowl that fits into the basket. Reserve the stock. Add the broccoli, onion, mushrooms, and ginger to the beef. Place the bowl into the basket. 5. Select AIR FRY, set the temperature to 200ºC, and set the time to 18 minutes. Select START/STOP to begin. 6. After about 12 minutes, check the beef and broccoli. If a food thermometer inserted into the beef registers at least 64ºC and the vegetables are tender, add the reserved stock and resume cooking for about 3 minutes until the sauce boils. If not, resume cooking for about 3 minutes before adding the reservedstock. 7. When the cooking is complete, serve immediately over hot cooked brown rice, if desired.

Italian Lamb Chops with Avocado Mayo

Prep time: 5 minutes | Cook time: 12 minutes | Serves 2

2 lamp chops	120 ml mayonnaise
2 teaspoons Italian herbs	1 tablespoon lemon juice
2 avocados	

1. Season the lamb chops with the Italian herbs, then set aside for 5 minutes. 2. Preheat the air fryer to 200°C and place the rack inside. 3. Put the chops on the rack and air fry for 12 minutes. 4. In the meantime, halve the avocados and open to remove the pits. Spoon the flesh into a blender. 5. Add the mayonnaise and lemon juice and pulse until a smooth consistency is achieved. 6. Take care when removing the chops from the air fryer, then plate up and serve with the avocado mayo.

Five-Spice Pork Belly

Prep time: 10 minutes | Cook time: 17 minutes | Serves 4

450 g unsalted pork belly	spice powder
2 teaspoons Chinese five-	

Sauce:

1 tablespoon coconut oil	¼ to 120 ml liquid or powdered sweetener
1 (1-inch) piece fresh ginger, peeled and grated	3 tablespoons wheat-free tamari
2 cloves garlic, minced	
120 ml beef or chicken stock	1 spring onion, sliced, plus more for garnish

1. Spray the air fryer basket with avocado oil. Preheat the air fryer to 200°C. 2. Cut the pork belly into ½-inch-thick slices and scason well on all sides with the five-spice powder. Place the slices in a single layer in the air fryer basket (if you're using a smaller air fryer, work in batches if necessary) and cook for 8 minutes, or until cooked to your liking, flipping halfway through. 3. While the pork belly cooks, make the sauce: Heat the coconut oil in a small saucepan over medium heat. Add the ginger and garlic and sauté for 1 minute, or until fragrant. Add the stock, sweetener, and tamari and simmer for 10 to 15 minutes, until thickened. Add the spring onion and cook for another minute, until the spring onion is softened. Taste and adjust the seasoning to your liking. 4. Transfer the pork belly to a large bowl. Pour the sauce over the pork belly and coat well. Place the pork belly slices on a serving platter and garnish with sliced spring onions. 5. Best served fresh. Store leftovers in an airtight container in the fridge for up to 4 days. Reheat in a preheated 200°C air fryer for 3 minutes, or until heated through.

Panko Pork Chops

Prep time: 10 minutes | Cook time: 12 minutes | Serves 4

4 boneless pork chops, excess fat trimmed	½ teaspoon granulated garlic
¼ teaspoon salt	½ teaspoon onion granules
2 eggs	
130 g panko bread crumbs	1 teaspoon chili powder
3 tablespoons grated Parmesan cheese	¼ teaspoon freshly ground black pepper
1½ teaspoons paprika	Olive oil spray

1. Sprinkle the pork chops with salt on both sides and let them sit while you prepare the seasonings and egg wash. 2. In a shallow medium bowl, beat the eggs. 3. In another shallow medium bowl, stir together the panko, Parmesan cheese, paprika, granulated garlic, onion granules, chili powder, and pepper. 4. Dip the pork chops in the egg and in the panko mixture to coat. Firmly press the crumbs onto the chops. 5. Insert the crisper plate into the basket and the basket into the unit. Preheat the unit by selecting AIR ROAST, setting the temperature to 200°C, and setting the time to 3 minutes. Select START/STOP to begin. 6. Once the unit is preheated, spray the crisper plate with olive oil. Place the pork chops into the basket and spray them with olive oil. 7. Select AIR ROAST, set the temperature to 200°C, and set the time to 12 minutes. Select START/STOP to begin. 8. After 6 minutes, flip the pork chops and spray them with more olive oil. Resume cooking. 9. When the cooking is complete, the chops should be golden and crispy and a food thermometer should register 64°C. Serve immediately.

Swedish Meatloaf

Prep time: 10 minutes | Cook time: 35 minutes | Serves 8

- 680 g beef mince (85% lean)
- 110 g pork mince
- 1 large egg (omit for egg-free)
- 120 g minced onions
- 60 ml tomato sauce
- 2 tablespoons mustard powder
- 2 cloves garlic, minced
- 2 teaspoons fine sea salt
- 1 teaspoon ground black pepper, plus more for garnish

Sauce:

- 120 g (1 stick) unsalted butter
- 120 g shredded Swiss or mild Cheddar cheese (about 60 g)
- 60 g cream cheese (60 ml), softened
- 80 ml beef stock
- ⅛ teaspoon ground nutmeg
- Halved cherry tomatoes, for serving (optional)

1. Preheat the air fryer to 200°C. 2. In a large bowl, combine the beef, pork, egg, onions, tomato sauce, mustard powder, garlic, salt, and pepper. Using your hands, mix until well combined. 3. Place the meatloaf mixture in a loaf pan and place it in the air fryer. Bake for 35 minutes, or until cooked through and the internal temperature reaches 64°C. Check the meatloaf after 25 minutes; if it's getting too brown on the top, cover it loosely with foil to prevent burning. 4. While the meatloaf cooks, make the sauce: Heat the butter in a saucepan over medium-high heat until it sizzles and brown flecks appear, stirring constantly to keep the butter from burning. Turn the heat down to low and whisk in the Swiss cheese, cream cheese, stock, and nutmeg. Simmer for at least 10 minutes. The longer it simmers, the more the flavours open up. 5. When the meatloaf is done, transfer it to a serving tray and pour the sauce over it. Garnish with ground black pepper and serve with cherry tomatoes, if desired. Allow the meatloaf to rest for 10 minutes before slicing so it doesn't crumble apart. 6. Store leftovers in an airtight container in the fridge for 3 days or in the freezer for up to a month. Reheat in a preheated 180°C air fryer for 4 minutes, or until heated through.

Ritzy Skirt Steak Fajitas

Prep time: 15 minutes | Cook time: 30 minutes | Serves 4

- 2 tablespoons olive oil
- 60 ml lime juice
- 1 clove garlic, minced
- ½ teaspoon ground cumin
- ½ teaspoon hot sauce
- ½ teaspoon salt
- 2 tablespoons chopped fresh coriander
- 450 g skirt steak
- 1 onion, sliced
- 1 teaspoon chili powder
- 1 red pepper, sliced
- 1 green pepper, sliced
- Salt and freshly ground black pepper, to taste
- 8 flour tortillas

Toppings:

- Shredded lettuce
- Crumbled feta or ricotta (or grated Cheddar cheese)
- Sliced black olives
- Diced tomatoes
- Sour cream
- Guacamole

1. Combine the olive oil, lime juice, garlic, cumin, hot sauce, salt and coriander in a shallow dish. Add the skirt steak and turn it over several times to coat all sides. Pierce the steak with a needle-style meat tenderizer or paring knife. Marinate the steak in the refrigerator for at least 3 hours, or overnight. When you are ready to cook, remove the steak from the refrigerator and let it sit at room temperature for 30 minutes. 2. Preheat the air fryer to 200°C. 3. Toss the onion slices with the chili powder and a little olive oil and transfer them to the air fryer basket. Air fry for 5 minutes. Add the red and green peppers to the air fryer basket with the onions, season with salt and pepper and air fry for 8 more minutes, until the onions and peppers are soft. Transfer the vegetables to a dish and cover with aluminum foil to keep warm. 4. Put the skirt steak in the air fryer basket and pour the marinade over the top. Air fry at 200°C for 12 minutes. Flip the steak over and air fry for an additional 5 minutes. Transfer the cooked steak to a cutting board and let the steak rest for a few minutes. If the peppers and onions need to be heated, return them to the air fryer for just 1 to 2 minutes. 5. Thinly slice the steak at an angle, cutting against the grain of the steak. Serve the steak with the onions and peppers, the warm tortillas and the fajita toppings on the side.

Parmesan Herb Filet Mignon

Prep time: 20 minutes | Cook time: 13 minutes | Serves 4

450 g filet mignon	rosemary
Sea salt and ground black pepper, to taste	1 teaspoon dried thyme
½ teaspoon cayenne pepper	1 tablespoon sesame oil
1 teaspoon dried basil	1 small-sized egg, well-whisked
1 teaspoon dried	120 g Parmesan cheese, grated

1. Season the filet mignon with salt, black pepper, cayenne pepper, basil, rosemary, and thyme. Brush with sesame oil. 2. Put the egg in a shallow plate. Now, place the Parmesan cheese in another plate. 3. Coat the filet mignon with the egg; then lay it into the Parmesan cheese. Set the air fryer to 180°C. 4. Cook for 10 to 13 minutes or until golden. Serve with mixed salad leaves and enjoy!

Greek Lamb Rack

Prep time: 5 minutes | Cook time: 10 minutes | Serves 4

60 g freshly squeezed lemon juice	garlic
1 teaspoon oregano	Salt and freshly ground black pepper, to taste
2 teaspoons minced fresh rosemary	2 to 4 tablespoons olive oil
1 teaspoon minced fresh thyme	1 lamb rib rack (7 to 8 ribs)
2 tablespoons minced	

1. Preheat the air fryer to 180°C. 2. In a small mixing bowl, combine the lemon juice, oregano, rosemary, thyme, garlic, salt, pepper, and olive oil and mix well. 3. Rub the mixture over the lamb, covering all the meat. Put the rack of lamb in the air fryer. Roast for 10 minutes. Flip the rack halfway through. 4. After 10 minutes, measure the internal temperature of the rack of lamb reaches at least 64°C. 5. Serve immediately.

Spinach and Beef Braciole

Prep time: 25 minutes | Cook time: 1 hour 32 minutes | Serves 4

½ onion, finely chopped	salt and freshly ground black pepper
1 teaspoon olive oil	475 g fresh spinach, chopped
80 ml red wine	
475 g crushed tomatoes	1 clove minced garlic
1 teaspoon Italian seasoning	120 g roasted red peppers, julienned
½ teaspoon garlic powder	120 g grated pecorino cheese
¼ teaspoon crushed red pepper flakes	
2 tablespoons chopped fresh parsley	60 g pine nuts, toasted and roughly chopped
2 bavette or skirt steaks (about 680 g)	2 tablespoons olive oil

1. Preheat the air fryer to 200°C. 2. Toss the onions and olive oil together in a baking tray or casserole dish. Air fry at 200°C for 5 minutes, stirring a couple times during the cooking process. Add the red wine, crushed tomatoes, Italian seasoning, garlic powder, red pepper flakes and parsley and stir. Cover the pan tightly with aluminum foil, lower the air fryer temperature to 180°C and continue to air fry for 15 minutes. 3. While the sauce is simmering, prepare the beef. Using a meat mallet, pound the beef until it is ¼-inch thick. Season both sides of the beef with salt and pepper. Combine the spinach, garlic, red peppers, pecorino cheese, pine nuts and olive oil in a medium bowl. Season with salt and freshly ground black pepper. Disperse the mixture over the steaks. Starting at one of the short ends, roll the beef around the filling, tucking in the sides as you roll to ensure the filling is completely enclosed. Secure the beef rolls with toothpicks. 4. Remove the baking tray with the sauce from the air fryer and set it aside. Preheat the air fryer to 200°C. 5. Brush or spray the beef rolls with a little olive oil and air fry at 200°C for 12 minutes, rotating the beef during the cooking process for even browning. When the beef is browned, submerge the rolls into the sauce in the baking tray, cover the pan with foil and return it to the air fryer. Reduce the temperature of the air fryer to 120°C and air fry for 60 minutes. 6. Remove the beef

rolls from the sauce. Cut each roll into slices and serve, ladling some sauce overtop.

Asian Glazed Meatballs
Prep time: 15 minutes | Cook time: 10 minutes per batch | Serves 4 to 6

1 large shallot, finely chopped	2 tablespoons soy sauce
2 cloves garlic, minced	Freshly ground black pepper, to taste
1 tablespoon grated fresh ginger	450 g beef mince
2 teaspoons fresh thyme, finely chopped	230 g pork mince
	3 egg yolks
355 g brown mushrooms, very finely chopped (a food processor works well here)	235 ml Thai sweet chili sauce (spring roll sauce)
	60 g toasted sesame seeds
	2 spring onionspring onions, sliced

1. Combine the shallot, garlic, ginger, thyme, mushrooms, soy sauce, freshly ground black pepper, beef and pork mince, and egg yolks in a bowl and mix the ingredients together. Gently shape the mixture into 24 balls, about the size of a golf ball. 2. Preheat the air fryer to 190ºC. 3. Working in batches, air fry the meatballs for 8 minutes, turning the meatballs over halfway through the cooking time. Drizzle some of the Thai sweet chili sauce on top of each meatball and return the basket to the air fryer, air frying for another 2 minutes. Reserve the remaining Thai sweet chili sauce for serving. 4. As soon as the meatballs are done, sprinkle with toasted sesame seeds and transfer them to a serving platter. Scatter the spring onionspring onions around and serve warm.

Bulgogi Burgers
Prep time: 30 minutes | Cook time: 10 minutes | Serves 4

Burgers:

450 g 85% lean beef mince	(Korean red chili paste)
60 g chopped spring onionspring onions	1 tablespoon dark soy sauce
2 tablespoons gochujang	2 teaspoons minced garlic
	2 teaspoons minced fresh ginger
2 teaspoons sugar	½ teaspoon coarse or flaky salt
1 tablespoon toasted sesame oil	

Gochujang Mayonnaise:

60 ml mayonnaise	1 tablespoon toasted sesame oil
60 g chopped spring onionspring onions	2 teaspoons sesame seeds
1 tablespoon gochujang (Korean red chili paste)	4 hamburger buns

1. For the burgers: In a large bowl, mix the ground beef, spring onionspring onions, gochujang, soy sauce, garlic, ginger, sugar, sesame oil, and salt. Marinate at room temperature for 30 minutes, or cover and refrigerate for up to 24 hours. 2. Divide the meat into four portions and form them into round patties. Make a slight depression in the middle of each patty with your thumb to prevent them from puffing up into a dome shape while cooking. 3. Place the patties in a single layer in the air fryer basket. Set the air fryer to 180ºC for 10 minutes. 4. Meanwhile, for the gochujang mayonnaise: Stir together the mayonnaise, spring onionspring onions, gochujang, sesame oil, and sesame seeds. 5. At the end of the cooking time, use a meat thermometer to ensure the burgers have reached an internal temperature of 72ºC (medium). 6. To serve, place the burgers on the buns and top with the mayonnaise.

Spicy Lamb Sirloin Chops
Prep time: 30 minutes | Cook time: 15 minutes | Serves 4

½ brown onion, coarsely chopped	1 teaspoon ground turmeric
4 coin-size slices peeled fresh ginger	½ to 1 teaspoon cayenne pepper
5 garlic cloves	½ teaspoon ground cardamom
1 teaspoon garam masala	
1 teaspoon ground fennel	1 teaspoon coarse or flaky salt
1 teaspoon ground cinnamon	450 g lamb sirloin chops

1. In a blender, combine the onion, ginger, garlic, garam masala, fennel, cinnamon, turmeric, cayenne, cardamom,

36 | Beef, Pork, and Lamb

and salt. Pulse until the onion is finely minced and the mixture forms a thick paste, 3 to 4 minutes. 2. Place the lamb chops in a large bowl. Slash the meat and fat with a sharp knife several times to allow the marinade to penetrate better. Add the spice paste to the bowl and toss the lamb to coat. Marinate at room temperature for 30 minutes or cover and refrigerate for up to 24 hours. 3. Place the lamb chops in a single layer in the air fryer basket. Set the air fryer to 160°C for 15 minutes, turning the chops halfway through the cooking time. Use a meat thermometer to ensure the lamb has reached an internal temperature of 64°C (medium-rare).

Chapter 6
Fish and Seafood

Fried Catfish Fillets

Prep time: 10 minutes | Cook time: 20 minutes | Serves 4

1 egg	seasoning
50 g finely ground cornmeal	¼ teaspoon garlic powder
20 g plain flour	¼ teaspoon freshly ground black pepper
¾ teaspoon salt	4 140 g catfish fillets, halved crosswise
1 teaspoon paprika	
1 teaspoon Old Bay	Olive oil spray

1. In a shallow bowl, beat the egg with 2 tablespoons water. 2. On a plate, stir together the cornmeal, flour, salt, paprika, Old Bay, garlic powder, and pepper. 3. Dip the fish into the egg mixture and into the cornmeal mixture to coat. Press the cornmeal mixture into the fish and gently shake off any excess. 4. Insert the crisper plate into the basket and the basket into the unit to 200°C. 5. Once the unit is preheated, place a baking paper liner into the basket. Place the coated fish on the liner and spray it with olive oil.. 6. Cook for 10 minutes, remove the basket and spray the fish with olive oil. Flip the fish and spray the other side with olive oil. Reinsert the basket to resume cooking. Check the fish after 7 minutes more. If the fish is golden and crispy and registers at least 64°C on a food thermometer, it is ready. If not, resume cooking. 8. When the cooking is complete, serve.

Asian Swordfish

Prep time: 10 minutes | Cook time: 6 to 11 minutes | Serves 4

4 swordfish steaks, 100 g each	ginger
½ teaspoon toasted sesame oil	½ teaspoon Chinese five-spice powder
1 jalapeño pepper, finely minced	⅛ teaspoon freshly ground black pepper
2 garlic cloves, grated	2 tablespoons freshly squeezed lemon juice
1 tablespoon grated fresh	

1. Place the swordfish steaks on a work surface and drizzle with the sesame oil. 2. In a small bowl, mix the jalapeño, garlic, ginger, five-spice powder, pepper, and lemon juice. Rub this mixture into the fish and let it stand for 10 minutes. 3. Roast the swordfish in the air fryer at 190°C for 6 to 11 minutes, or until the swordfish reaches an internal temperature of at least 60°C on a meat thermometer. Serve immediately.

Cornmeal-Crusted Trout Fingers

Prep time: 15 minutes | Cook time: 6 minutes | Serves 2

70 g yellow cornmeal, medium or finely ground (not coarse)	fillets, cut into strips 1 inch wide and 3 inches long
20 g plain flour	3 large eggs, lightly beaten
1½ teaspoons baking powder	Cooking spray
1 teaspoon kosher or coarse sea salt, plus more as needed	115 g mayonnaise
	2 tablespoons capers, rinsed and finely chopped
½ teaspoon freshly ground black pepper, plus more as needed	1 tablespoon fresh tarragon
⅛ teaspoon cayenne pepper	1 teaspoon fresh lemon juice, plus lemon wedges, for serving
340 g skinless trout	

1. Preheat the air fryer to 200°C. 2. In a large bowl, whisk together the cornmeal, flour, baking powder, salt, black pepper, and cayenne. Dip the trout strips in the egg, then toss them in the cornmeal mixture until fully coated. Transfer the trout to a rack set over a baking sheet and liberally spray all over with cooking spray. 3. Transfer half the fish to the air fryer and air fry until the fish is cooked through and golden brown, about 6 minutes. Transfer the fish sticks to a plate and repeat with the remaining fish. 4. Meanwhile, in a bowl, whisk together the mayonnaise, capers, tarragon, and lemon juice. Season the tartar sauce with salt and black pepper. 5. Serve the trout fingers hot along with the tartar sauce and lemon wedges.

Snapper with Shallot and Tomato

Prep time: 20 minutes | Cook time: 15 minutes | Serves 2

2 snapper fillets	1 tomato, sliced
1 shallot, peeled and sliced	1 tablespoon olive oil
2 garlic cloves, halved	¼ teaspoon freshly ground black pepper
1 bell pepper, sliced	½ teaspoon paprika
1 small-sized serrano pepper, sliced	Sea salt, to taste
	2 bay leaves

1. Place two baking paper sheets on a working surface. Place the fish in the center of one side of the baking paper. 2. Top with the shallot, garlic, peppers, and tomato. Drizzle olive oil over the fish and vegetables. Season with black pepper, paprika, and salt. Add the bay leaves. 3. Fold over the other half of the baking paper. Now, fold the paper around the edges tightly and create a half moon shape, sealing the fish inside. 4. Cook in the preheated air fryer at 200°C for 15 minutes. Serve warm.

Chilean Sea Bass with Olive Relish

Prep time: 10 minutes | Cook time: 10 minutes | Serves 2

Olive oil spray	coarse sea salt
2 (170 g) Chilean sea bass fillets or other firm-fleshed white fish	½ teaspoon black pepper
	60 g pitted green olives, diced
3 tablespoons extra-virgin olive oil	10 g finely diced onion
	1 teaspoon chopped capers
½ teaspoon ground cumin	
½ teaspoon kosher or	

1. Spray the air fryer basket with the olive oil spray. Drizzle the fillets with the olive oil and sprinkle with the cumin, salt, and pepper. Place the fish in the air fryer basket. Set the air fryer to 160°C for 10 minutes, or until the fish flakes easily with a fork. 2. Meanwhile, in a small bowl, stir together the olives, onion, and capers. 3. Serve the fish topped with the relish.

Fish Croquettes with Lemon-Dill Aioli

Prep time: 15 minutes | Cook time: 10 minutes | Serves 4

Croquettes:

3 large eggs, divided	minced
340 g raw cod fillet, flaked apart with two forks	60 g breadcrumbs plus 2 tablespoons, divided
	1 teaspoon fresh lemon juice
60 ml skimmed milk	
190 g boxed instant mashed potatoes	1 teaspoon kosher or coarse sea salt
2 teaspoons olive oil	½ teaspoon dried thyme
8 g chopped fresh dill	¼ teaspoon freshly ground black pepper
1 shallot, minced	
1 large garlic clove,	Cooking spray

Lemon-Dill Aioli:

5 tablespoons mayonnaise	1 tablespoon chopped fresh dill
Juice of ½ lemon	

1. For the croquettes: In a medium bowl, lightly beat 2 of the eggs. Add the fish, milk, instant mashed potatoes, olive oil, dill, shallot, and garlic, 2 tablespoons of the bread crumbs, lemon juice, salt, thyme, and pepper. Mix to thoroughly combine. Place in the refrigerator for 30 minutes. 2. For the lemon-dill aioli: In a small bowl, combine the mayonnaise, lemon juice, and dill. Set aside. 3. Measure out about 3½ tablespoons of the fish mixture and gently roll in your hands to form a log about 3 inches long. Repeat to make a total of 12 logs. 4. Beat the remaining egg in a small bowl. Place the remaining ¾ cup bread crumbs in a separate bowl. Dip the croquettes in the egg, then coat in the bread crumbs, gently pressing to adhere. Place on a work surface and spray both sides with cooking spray. 5. Preheat the air fryer to 180°C. 6. Working in batches, arrange a single layer of the croquettes in the air fryer basket. Air fry for about 10 minutes, flipping halfway, until golden. 7. Serve with the aioli for dipping.

Crab-Stuffed Avocado Boats

Prep time: 5 minutes | Cook time: 7 minutes | Serves 4

2 medium avocados, halved and pitted	seasoning
230 g cooked crab meat	2 tablespoons peeled and diced yellow onion
¼ teaspoon Old Bay	2 tablespoons mayonnaise

1. Scoop out avocado flesh in each avocado half, leaving ½ inch around edges to form a shell. Chop scooped-out avocado. 2. In a medium bowl, combine crab meat, Old Bay seasoning, onion, mayonnaise, and chopped avocado. Place ¼ mixture into each avocado shell. 3. Place avocado boats into ungreased air fryer basket. Adjust the temperature to 180°C and air fry for 7 minutes. Avocado will be browned on the top and mixture will be bubbling when done. Serve warm.

Cheesy Tuna Patties

Prep time: 5 minutes | Cook time: 17 to 18 minutes | Serves 4

Tuna Patties:

455 g canned tuna, drained	1 cup grated Romano cheese
1 egg, whisked	Sea salt and ground black pepper, to taste
2 tablespoons shallots, minced	1 tablespoon sesame oil
1 garlic clove, minced	

Cheese Sauce:

1 tablespoon butter	2 tablespoons grated Cheddar cheese
240 ml beer	

1. Mix together the canned tuna, whisked egg, shallots, garlic, cheese, salt, and pepper in a large bowl and stir to incorporate. 2. Divide the tuna mixture into four equal portions and form each portion into a patty with your hands. Refrigerate the patties for 2 hours. 3. When ready, brush both sides of each patty with sesame oil. 4. Preheat the air fryer to 180°C. 5. Place the patties in the air fryer basket and bake for 14 minutes, flipping the patties halfway through, or until lightly browned and cooked through. 6. Meanwhile, melt the butter in a pan over medium heat. 7. Pour in the beer and whisk constantly, or until it begins to bubble. 8. Add the grated Colby cheese and mix well. Continue cooking for 3 to 4 minutes, or until the cheese melts. Remove the patties from the basket to a plate. Drizzle them with the cheese sauce and serve immediately.

Tuna Avocado Bites

Prep time: 10 minutes | Cook time: 7 minutes | Makes 12 bites

280 g canned tuna, drained	mashed
60 ml full-fat mayonnaise	25 g blanched finely ground almond flour, divided
1 stalk celery, chopped	
1 medium avocado, peeled, pitted, and	2 teaspoons coconut oil

1. In a large bowl, mix tuna, mayonnaise, celery, and mashed avocado. Form the mixture into balls. 2. Roll balls in almond flour and spritz with coconut oil. Place balls into the air fryer basket. 3. Adjust the temperature to 200°C and set the timer for 7 minutes. 4. Gently turn tuna bites after 5 minutes. Serve warm.

Crab Cakes

Prep time: 10 minutes | Cook time: 10 minutes | Serves 4

2 cans lump crab meat, 170 g each	½ tablespoon lemon juice
¼ cup blanched finely ground almond flour	½ medium green bell pepper, seeded and chopped
1 large egg	235 g chopped spring onion
2 tablespoons full-fat mayonnaise	½ teaspoon Old Bay seasoning
½ teaspoon Dijon mustard	

1. In a large bowl, combine all ingredients. Form into four balls and flatten into patties. Place patties into the air fryer basket. 2. Adjust the temperature to 180°C and air fry for 10 minutes. 3. Flip patties halfway through the cooking time. Serve warm.

Fish and Seafood | 41

Salmon Spring Rolls

Prep time: 20 minutes | Cook time: 8 to 10 minutes | Serves 4

230 g salmon fillet	thinly sliced
1 teaspoon toasted sesame oil	1 carrot, shredded
1 onion, sliced	10 g chopped fresh flat-leaf parsley
8 rice paper wrappers	15 g chopped fresh basil
1 yellow bell pepper,	

1. Put the salmon in the air fryer basket and drizzle with the sesame oil. Add the onion. Air fry at 190ºC for 8 to 10 minutes, or until the salmon just flakes when tested with a fork and the onion is tender. 2. Meanwhile, fill a small shallow bowl with warm water. One at a time, dip the rice paper wrappers into the water and place on a work surface. 3. Top each wrapper with one-eighth each of the salmon and onion mixture, yellow bell pepper, carrot, parsley, and basil. Roll up the wrapper, folding in the sides, to enclose the ingredients. 4. If you like, bake in the air fryer at 190ºC for 7 to 9 minutes, until the rolls are crunchy. Cut the rolls in half to serve.

South Indian Fried Fish

Prep time: 20 minutes | Cook time: 8 minutes | Serves 4

2 tablespoons olive oil	coarse sea salt
2 tablespoons fresh lime or lemon juice	¼ to ½ teaspoon cayenne pepper
1 teaspoon minced fresh ginger	455 g tilapia fillets (2 to 3 fillets)
1 clove garlic, minced	Olive oil spray
1 teaspoon ground turmeric	Lime or lemon wedges (optional)
½ teaspoon kosher or	

1. In a large bowl, combine the oil, lime juice, ginger, garlic, turmeric, salt, and cayenne. Stir until well combined; set aside. 2. Cut each tilapia fillet into three or four equal-size pieces. Add the fish to the bowl and gently mix until all of the fish is coated in the marinade. Marinate for 10 to 15 minutes at room temperature. (Don't marinate any longer or the acid in the lime juice will "cook" the fish.) 3. Spray the air fryer basket with olive oil spray. Place the fish in the basket and spray the fish. Set the air fryer to 160ºC for 3 minutes to partially cook the fish. Set the air fryer to 200ºC for 5 minutes to finish cooking and crisp up the fish. (Thinner pieces of fish will cook faster so you may want to check at the 3-minute mark of the second cooking time and remove those that are cooked through, and then add them back toward the end of the second cooking time to crisp.) 4. Carefully remove the fish from the basket. Serve hot, with lemon wedges if desired.

Thai Prawn Skewers with Peanut Dipping Sauce

Prep time: 15 minutes | Cook time: 6 minutes | Serves 2

Salt and pepper, to taste	6 (6-inch) wooden skewers
340 g extra-large prawns, peeled and deveined	3 tablespoons creamy peanut butter
1 tablespoon vegetable oil	3 tablespoons hot tap water
1 teaspoon honey	1 tablespoon chopped fresh coriander
½ teaspoon grated lime zest plus 1 tablespoon juice, plus lime wedges for serving	1 teaspoon fish sauce

1. Preheat the air fryer to 200ºC. 2. Dissolve 2 tablespoons salt in 1 litre cold water in a large container. Add prawns, cover, and refrigerate for 15 minutes. 3. Remove prawns from brine and pat dry with paper towels. Whisk oil, honey, lime zest, and ¼ teaspoon pepper together in a large bowl. Add prawns and toss to coat. Thread prawns onto skewers, leaving about ¼ inch between each prawns (3 or 4 prawns per skewer). 4. Arrange 3 skewers in air fryer basket, parallel to each other and spaced evenly apart. Arrange remaining 3 skewers on top, perpendicular to the bottom layer. Air fry until prawns are opaque throughout, 6 to 8 minutes, flipping and rotating skewers halfway through cooking. 5. Whisk peanut butter, hot tap water, lime juice, coriander, and fish sauce together in a bowl until smooth. Serve skewers with peanut dipping sauce and lime wedges.

Tandoori Prawns

Prep time: 25 minutes | Cook time: 6 minutes | Serves 4

455 g jumbo raw prawns (21 to 25 count), peeled and deveined	1 teaspoon garam masala
	1 teaspoon smoked paprika
1 tablespoon minced fresh ginger	1 teaspoon kosher or coarse sea salt
3 cloves garlic, minced	½ to 1 teaspoon cayenne pepper
5 g chopped fresh coriander or parsley, plus more for garnish	2 tablespoons olive oil (for Paleo) or melted ghee
1 teaspoon ground turmeric	2 teaspoons fresh lemon juice

1. In a large bowl, combine the prawns, ginger, garlic, coriander, turmeric, garam masala, paprika, salt, and cayenne. Toss well to coat. Add the oil or ghee and toss again. Marinate at room temperature for 15 minutes, or cover and refrigerate for up to 8 hours. 2. Place the prawns in a single layer in the air fryer basket. Set the air fryer to 160°C for 6 minutes. Transfer the prawns to a serving platter. Cover and let the prawns finish cooking in the residual heat, about 5 minutes. 3. Sprinkle the prawns with the lemon juice and toss to coat. Garnish with additional cilantro and serve.

Fish Cakes

Prep time: 30 minutes | Cook time: 10 to 12 minutes | Serves 4

1 large russet potato, mashed	1 large egg
	50 g potato starch
340 g cod or other white fish	30 g panko breadcrumbs
	1 tablespoon fresh chopped chives
Salt and pepper, to taste	
Olive or vegetable oil for misting or cooking spray	2 tablespoons minced onion

1. Peel potatoes, cut into cubes, and cook on stovetop till soft. 2. Salt and pepper raw fish to taste. Mist with oil or cooking spray, and air fry at 180°C for 6 to 8 minutes, until fish flakes easily. If fish is crowded, rearrange halfway through cooking to ensure all pieces cook evenly. 3. Transfer fish to a plate and break apart to cool. 4. Beat egg in a shallow dish. 5. Place potato starch in another shallow dish, and panko crumbs in a third dish. 6. When potatoes are done, drain in colander and rinse with cold water. 7. In a large bowl, mash the potatoes and stir in the chives and onion. Add salt and pepper to taste, then stir in the fish. 8. If needed, stir in a tablespoon of the beaten egg to help bind the mixture. 9. Shape into 8 small, fat patties. Dust lightly with potato starch, dip in egg, and roll in panko crumbs. Spray both sides with oil or cooking spray. 10. Air fry for 10 to 12 minutes, until golden brown and crispy.

Crustless Prawn Quiche

Prep time: 15 minutes | Cook time: 20 minutes | Serves 2

Vegetable oil	onions
4 large eggs	1 teaspoon sweet smoked paprika
120 ml single cream	
110 g raw prawns, chopped	1 teaspoon Herbes de Provence
120 g shredded Parmesan or Swiss cheese	1 teaspoon black pepper
	½ to 1 teaspoon kosher or coarse sea salt
235 g chopped spring	

1. Generously grease a baking pan with vegetable oil. (Be sure to grease the pan well, the proteins in eggs stick something fierce. Alternatively, line the bottom of the pan with baking paper cut to fit and spray the baking paper and sides of the pan generously with vegetable oil spray.) 2. In a large bowl, beat together the eggs and single cream. Add the prawns, 90 g of the cheese, the scallions, paprika, Herbes de Provence, pepper, and salt. Stir with a fork to thoroughly combine. Pour the egg mixture into the prepared pan. 3. Place the pan in the air fryer basket. Set the air fryer to 150°C for 20 minutes. After 17 minutes, sprinkle the remaining 30 g cheese on top and cook for the remaining 3 minutes, or until the cheese has melted, the eggs are set, and a toothpick inserted into the center comes out clean. 4. Serve the quiche warm or at room temperature.

Fish Tacos with Jalapeño-Lime Sauce

Prep time: 25 minutes | Cook time: 7 to 10 minutes | Serves 4

Fish Tacos:

455 g firm white fish fillets	¼ teaspoon smoked paprika
¼ teaspoon cumin	1 teaspoon oil
¼ teaspoon coriander	Cooking spray
⅛ teaspoon ground red pepper	6 to 8 corn or flour tortillas (6-inch size)
1 tablespoon lime zest	

Jalapeño-Lime Sauce:

120 ml sour cream	½ teaspoon minced jalapeño (flesh only)
1 tablespoon lime juice	¼ teaspoon cumin
¼ teaspoon grated lime zest	

Napa Cabbage Garnish:

90 g shredded Savoy cabbage	bell pepper
40 g sliced red or green	30 g sliced onion

1. Slice the fish fillets into strips approximately ½-inch thick. 2. Put the strips into a sealable plastic bag along with the cumin, coriander, red pepper, lime zest, smoked paprika, and oil. Massage seasonings into the fish until evenly distributed. 3. Spray the air fryer basket with nonstick cooking spray and place seasoned fish inside. 4. Air fry at 200ºC for approximately 5 minutes. Shake basket to distribute fish. Cook an additional 2 to 5 minutes, until fish flakes easily. 5. While the fish is cooking, prepare the Jalapeño-Lime Sauce by mixing the sour cream, lime juice, lime zest, jalapeño, and cumin together to make a smooth sauce. Set aside. 6. Mix the cabbage, bell pepper, and onion together and set aside. 7. To warm refrigerated tortillas, wrap in damp paper towels and microwave for 30 to 60 seconds. 8. To serve, spoon some of fish into a warm tortilla. Add one or two tablespoons Napa Cabbage Garnish and drizzle with Jalapeño-Lime Sauce.

Crunchy Air Fried Cod Fillets

Prep time: 10 minutes | Cook time: 12 minutes | Serves 2

20 g panko bread crumbs	parsley
1 teaspoon vegetable oil	1 tablespoon mayonnaise
1 small shallot, minced	1 large egg yolk
1 small garlic clove, minced	¼ teaspoon grated lemon zest, plus lemon wedges for serving
½ teaspoon minced fresh thyme	2 (230 g) skinless cod fillets, 1¼ inches thick
Salt and pepper, to taste	
1 tablespoon minced fresh	Vegetable oil spray

1. Preheat the air fryer to 150ºC. 2. Make foil sling for air fryer basket by folding 1 long sheet of aluminum foil so it is 4 inches wide. Lay sheet of foil widthwise across basket, pressing foil into and up sides of basket. Fold excess foil as needed so that edges of foil are flush with top of basket. Lightly spray the foil and basket with vegetable oil spray. 3. Toss the panko with the oil in a bowl until evenly coated. Stir in the shallot, garlic, thyme, ¼ teaspoon salt, and ⅛ teaspoon pepper. Microwave, stirring frequently, until the panko is light golden brown, about 2 minutes. Transfer to a shallow dish and let cool slightly; stir in the parsley. Whisk the mayonnaise, egg yolk, lemon zest, and ⅛ teaspoon pepper together in another bowl. 4. Pat the cod dry with paper towels and season with salt and pepper. Arrange the fillets, skinned-side down, on plate and brush tops evenly with mayonnaise mixture. (Tuck thinner tail ends of fillets under themselves as needed to create uniform pieces.) Working with 1 fillet at a time, dredge the coated side in panko mixture, pressing gently to adhere. Arrange the fillets, crumb-side up, on sling in the prepared basket, spaced evenly apart. 5. Bake for 12 to 16 minutes, using a sling to rotate fillets halfway through cooking. Using a sling, carefully remove cod from air fryer. Serve with the lemon wedges.

Roasted Halibut Steaks with Parsley

Prep time: 5 minutes | Cook time: 10 minutes | Serves 4

455 g halibut steaks	1 tablespoon freshly squeezed lemon juice
60 ml vegetable oil	
2½ tablespoons Worcester sauce	1 tablespoon fresh parsley leaves, coarsely chopped
2 tablespoons honey	Salt and pepper, to taste
2 tablespoons vermouth or white wine vinegar	1 teaspoon dried basil

1. Preheat the air fryer to 200°C. 2. Put all the ingredients in a large mixing dish and gently stir until the fish is coated evenly. 3. Transfer the fish to the air fryer basket and roast for 10 minutes, flipping the fish halfway through, or until the fish reaches an internal temperature of at least 64°C on a meat thermometer. 4. Let the fish cool for 5 minutes and serve.

Sea Bass with Potato Scales

Prep time: 10 minutes | Cook time: 10 minutes | Serves 2

2 fillets of sea bass, 170- to 230 g each	potatoes, very thinly sliced into rounds
Salt and freshly ground black pepper, to taste	Olive oil
60 ml mayonnaise	½ clove garlic, crushed into a paste
2 teaspoons finely chopped lemon zest	1 tablespoon capers, drained and rinsed
1 teaspoon chopped fresh thyme	1 tablespoon olive oil
2 Fingerling, or new	1 teaspoon lemon juice, to taste

1. Preheat the air fryer to 200°C. 2. Season the fish well with salt and freshly ground black pepper. Mix the mayonnaise, lemon zest and thyme together in a small bowl. Spread a thin layer of the mayonnaise mixture on both fillets. Start layering rows of potato slices onto the fish fillets to simulate the fish scales. The second row should overlap the first row slightly. Dabbing a little more mayonnaise along the upper edge of the row of potatoes where the next row overlaps will help the potato slices stick. Press the potatoes onto the fish to secure them well and season again with salt. Brush or spray the potato layer with olive oil. 3. Transfer the fish to the air fryer and air fry for 8 to 10 minutes, depending on the thickness of your fillets. 1-inch of fish should take 10 minutes at 200°C. 4. While the fish is cooking, add the garlic, capers, olive oil and lemon juice to the remaining mayonnaise mixture to make the caper aïoli. 5. Serve the fish warm with a dollop of the aïoli on top or on the side.

Cod Tacos with Mango Salsa

Prep time: 15 minutes | Cook time: 17 minutes | Serves 4

1 mango, peeled and diced	120 ml Mexican beer
	1 egg
1 small jalapeño pepper, diced	75 g cornflour
	90 g plain flour
½ red bell pepper, diced	½ teaspoon ground cumin
½ red onion, minced	¼ teaspoon chilli powder
Pinch chopped fresh cilantro	455 g cod, cut into 4 pieces
Juice of ½ lime	Olive oil spray
¼ teaspoon salt	4 corn tortillas, or flour tortillas, at room temperature
¼ teaspoon ground black pepper	

1. In a small bowl, stir together the mango, jalapeño, red bell pepper, red onion, cilantro, lime juice, salt, and pepper. Set aside. 2. In a medium bowl, whisk the beer and egg. 3. In another medium bowl, stir together the cornflour, flour, cumin, and chilli powder. 4. Insert the crisper plate into the basket and the basket into the unit. Preheat the unit to 190°C. 5. Dip the fish pieces into the egg mixture and in the flour mixture to coat completely. 6. Once the unit is preheated, place a baking paper liner into the basket. Place the fish on the liner in a single layer. 7. Cook for about 9 minutes, spray the fish with olive oil. Reinsert the basket to resume cooking. 8. When the cooking is complete, the fish should be golden and crispy. Place the pieces in the tortillas, top with the mango salsa, and serve.

Fish and Seafood | 45

Sole and Cauliflower Fritters

Prep time: 5 minutes | Cook time: 24 minutes | Serves 2

230 g sole fillets	1 tablespoon olive oil
230 g mashed cauliflower	1 tablespoon coconut aminos or tamari
75 g red onion, chopped	½ teaspoon scotch bonnet pepper, minced
1 bell pepper, finely chopped	½ teaspoon paprika
1 egg, beaten	Salt and white pepper, to taste
2 garlic cloves, minced	Cooking spray
2 tablespoons fresh parsley, chopped	

1. Preheat the air fryer to 200°C. Spray the air fryer basket with cooking spray. 2. Place the sole fillets in the basket and air fry for 10 minutes, flipping them halfway through. 3. When the fillets are done, transfer them to a large bowl. Mash the fillets into flakes. Add the remaining ingredients and stir to combine. 4. Make the fritters: Scoop out 2 tablespoons of the fish mixture and shape into a patty about ½ inch thick with your hands. Repeat with the remaining fish mixture. 5. Arrange the patties in the air fryer basket and bake for 14 minutes, flipping the patties halfway through, or until they are golden brown and cooked through. 6. Cool for 5 minutes and serve on a plate.

Herbed Prawns Pita

Prep time: 5 minutes | Cook time: 8 minutes | Serves 4

455 g medium prawns, peeled and deveined	¼ teaspoon black pepper
2 tablespoons olive oil	4 whole wheat pitas
1 teaspoon dried oregano	110 g feta cheese, crumbled
½ teaspoon dried thyme	75 g shredded lettuce
½ teaspoon garlic powder	1 tomato, diced
¼ teaspoon onion powder	45 g black olives, sliced
½ teaspoon salt	1 lemon

1. Preheat the oven to 190°C. 2. In a medium bowl, combine the prawns with the olive oil, oregano, thyme, garlic powder, onion powder, salt, and black pepper. 3. Pour prawns in a single layer in the air fryer basket and roast for 6 to 8 minutes, or until cooked through. 4. Remove from the air fryer and divide into warmed pitas with feta, lettuce, tomato, olives, and a squeeze of lemon.

One-Pot Prawn Fried Rice

Prep time: 10 minutes | Cook time: 25 minutes | Serves 4

Prawns:

1 teaspoon cornflour	455 g jumbo raw prawns (21 to 25 count), peeled and deveined
½ teaspoon kosher or coarse sea salt	
¼ teaspoon black pepper	

Rice:

200 g cold cooked rice	3 tablespoons toasted sesame oil
140 g frozen peas and carrots, thawed	1 tablespoon soy sauce
235 g chopped spring onions (white and green parts)	½ teaspoon kosher or coarse sea salt
	1 teaspoon black pepper

Eggs:

2 large eggs, beaten	coarse sea salt
¼ teaspoon kosher or	¼ teaspoon black pepper

1. For the prawns: In a small bowl, whisk together the cornflour, salt, and pepper until well combined. Place the prawns in a large bowl and sprinkle the seasoned cornflour over. Toss until well coated; set aside. 2. For the rice: In a baking pan, combine the rice, peas and carrots, spring onions, sesame oil, soy sauce, salt, and pepper. Toss and stir until well combined. 3. Place the pan in the air fryer basket. Set the air fryer to 180°C for 15 minutes, stirring and tossing the rice halfway through the cooking time. 4. Place the prawns on top of the rice. Cook for 5 minutes. 5. Meanwhile, for the eggs: In a medium bowl, beat the eggs with the salt and pepper. 6. Open the air fryer and pour the eggs over the prawns and rice mixture. Cook for 5 minutes. 7. Remove the pan from the air fryer. Stir to break up the rice and mix in the eggs and prawns.

Garlic Butter Prawns Scampi

Prep time: 5 minutes | Cook time: 8 minutes | Serves 4

Sauce:

60 g unsalted butter	1 tablespoon lemon juice
2 tablespoons fish stock or chicken broth	1 tablespoon chopped fresh parsley, plus more for garnish
2 cloves garlic, minced	
2 tablespoons chopped fresh basil leaves	1 teaspoon red pepper flakes

Prawns:

455 g large prawns, peeled and deveined, tails removed
Fresh basil sprigs, for garnish

1. Preheat the air fryer to 180°C. 2. Put all the ingredients for the sauce in a baking pan and stir to incorporate. 3. Transfer the baking pan to the air fryer and air fry for 3 minutes, or until the sauce is heated through. 4. Once done, add the prawns to the baking pan, flipping to coat in the sauce. 5. Return to the air fryer and cook for another 5 minutes, or until the prawns are pink and opaque. Stir the prawns twice during cooking. 6. Serve garnished with the parsley and basil sprigs.

Chapter 7
Snacks and Appetizers

Spicy Tortilla Chips

Prep time: 5 minutes | Cook time: 8 to 12 minutes | Serves 4

½ teaspoon cumin powder	Pinch cayenne pepper
½ teaspoon paprika	8 (6-inch) sweetcorn tortillas, each cut into 6 wedges
½ teaspoon chili powder	
½ teaspoon salt	Cooking spray

1. Preheat the air fryer to 190°C. Lightly spritz the air fryer basket with cooking spray. 2. Stir together the cumin, paprika, chili powder, salt, and pepper in a small bowl. 3. Working in batches, arrange the tortilla wedges in the air fryer basket in a single layer. Lightly mist them with cooking spray. Sprinkle some seasoning mixture on top of the tortilla wedges. 4. Air fry for 4 to 6 minutes, shaking the basket halfway through, or until the chips are lightly browned and crunchy. 5. Repeat with the remaining tortilla wedges and seasoning mixture. 6. Let the tortilla chips cool for 5 minutes and serve.

Turkey Burger Sliders

Prep time: 10 minutes | Cook time: 5 to 7 minutes | Makes 8 sliders

450 g finely chopped turkey	onions
¼ teaspoon curry powder	60 g slivered green or red pepper
1 teaspoon Hoisin sauce	100 g fresh diced pineapple
½ teaspoon salt	
8 mini rolls	Light soft white cheese
60 g thinly sliced red	

1. Combine turkey, curry powder, Hoisin sauce, and salt and mix together well. 2. Shape turkey mixture into 8 small burger patties. 3. Place burger patties in air fryer basket and air fry at 180°C for 5 to 7 minutes, until burger patties are well done, and the juices are clear. 4. Place each patty on the bottom half of a slider roll and top with onions, peppers, and pineapple. Spread the remaining bun halves with soft white cheese to taste, place on top, and serve.

Soft white cheese Stuffed Jalapeño Chillies Poppers

Prep time: 12 minutes | Cook time: 6 to 8 minutes | Serves 10

227 g soft white cheese, at room temperature	1 teaspoon chili powder
80 g panko breadcrumbs, divided	10 jalapeño chillies chillies, halved and seeded
2 tablespoons fresh parsley, minced	Cooking oil spray

1. In a small bowl, whisk the soft white cheese, 40 g of panko, the parsley, and chili powder until combined. Stuff the cheese mixture into the jalapeño chillies halves. 2. Sprinkle the tops of the stuffed jalapeño chillies with the remaining 40 g of panko and press it lightly into the filling. 3. Insert the crisper plate into the basket and the basket into the unit. Preheat the unit by selecting AIR FRY, setting the temperature to 190°C, and setting the time to 3 minutes. Select START/STOP to begin. 4. Once the unit is preheated, spray the crisper plate with cooking oil. Place the poppers into the basket. 5. Select AIR FRY, set the temperature to 190°C, and set the time to 8 minutes. Select START/STOP to begin. 6. After 6 minutes, check the poppers. If they are softened and the cheese is melted, they are done. If not, resume cooking. 7. When the cooking is complete, serve warm.

Kale Chips with Sesame

Prep time: 15 minutes | Cook time: 8 minutes | Serves 5

2L deribbed kale leaves, torn into 2-inch pieces	¼ teaspoon garlic powder
1½ tablespoons olive oil	½ teaspoon paprika
¾ teaspoon chili powder	2 teaspoons sesame seeds

1. Preheat air fryer to 180°C. 2. In a large bowl, toss the kale with the olive oil, chili powder, garlic powder, paprika, and sesame seeds until well coated. 3. Put the kale in the air fryer basket and air fry for 8 minutes, flipping the kale twice during cooking, or until the kale is crispy. 4. Serve warm.

Lemon Prawns with Garlic Olive Oil

Prep time: 5 minutes | Cook time: 6 minutes | Serves 4

340 g medium prawns, cleaned and deveined	½ teaspoon salt
60 ml plus 2 tablespoons olive oil, divided	¼ teaspoon red pepper flakes
Juice of ½ lemon	Lemon wedges, for serving (optional)
3 garlic cloves, minced and divided	Marinara sauce, for dipping (optional)

1. Preheat the air fryer to 190ºC. 2. In a large bowl, combine the prawns with 2 tablespoons of the olive oil, as well as the lemon juice, ⅓ of the minced garlic, salt, and red pepper flakes. Toss to coat the prawns well. 3. In a small ramekin, combine the remaining 60 ml of olive oil and the remaining minced garlic. 4. Tear off a 12-by-12-inch sheet of aluminium foil. Pour the prawns into the centre of the foil, then fold the sides up and crimp the edges so that it forms an aluminium foil bowl that is open on top. Place this packet into the air fryer basket. 5. Roast the prawns for 4 minutes, then open the air fryer and place the ramekin with oil and garlic in the basket beside the prawns packet. Cook for 2 more minutes. 6. Transfer the prawns on a serving plate or platter with the ramekin of garlic olive oil on the side for dipping. You may also serve with lemon wedges and marinara sauce, if desired.

Authentic Scotch Eggs

Prep time: 15 minutes | Cook time: 11 to 13 minutes | Serves 6

680 g bulk lean chicken or turkey sausage	divided
3 raw eggs, divided	65 g plain flour
100 g dried breadcrumbs,	6 hardboiled eggs, peeled
	Cooking oil spray

1. In a large bowl, combine the chicken sausage, 1 raw egg, and 40 g of breadcrumbs and mix well. Divide the mixture into 6 pieces and flatten each into a long oval. 2. In a shallow dish, beat the remaining 2 raw eggs. 3. Place the flour in a small bowl. 4. Place the remaining 80 g of breadcrumbs in a second small bowl. 5. Roll each hardboiled egg in the flour and wrap one of the chicken sausage pieces around each egg to encircle it completely. 6. One at a time, roll the encased eggs in the flour, dip in the beaten eggs, and finally dip in the breadcrumbs to coat. 7. Insert the crisper plate into the basket and the basket into the unit. Preheat the unit by selecting AIR FRY, setting the temperature to 190ºC, and setting the time to 3 minutes. Select START/STOP to begin. 8. Once the unit is preheated, spray the crisper plate with cooking oil. Place the eggs in a single layer into the basket and spray them with oil. 9. Select AIR FRY, set the temperature to 190ºC, and set the time to 13 minutes. Select START/STOP to begin. 10. After about 6 minutes, use tongs to turn the eggs and spray them with more oil. Resume cooking for 5 to 7 minutes more, or until the chicken is thoroughly cooked and the Scotch eggs are browned. 11. When the cooking is complete, serve warm.

Bruschetta with Basil Pesto

Prep time: 10 minutes | Cook time: 5 to 11 minutes | Serves 4

8 slices French bread, ½ inch thick	120 g basil pesto
2 tablespoons softened butter	240 g chopped cherry tomatoes
120 g shredded mozzarella cheese cheese	2 spring onions, thinly sliced

1. Preheat the air fryer to 180ºC. 2. Spread the bread with the butter and place butter-side up in the air fryer basket. Bake for 3 to 5 minutes, or until the bread is light golden. 3. Remove the bread from the basket and top each piece with some of the cheese. Return to the basket in 2 batches and bake for 1 to 3 minutes, or until the cheese melts. 4. Meanwhile, combine the pesto, tomatoes, and spring onions in a small bowl. 5. When the cheese has melted, remove the bread from the air fryer and place on a serving plate. Top each slice with some of the pesto mixture and serve.

Mozzarella Cheese Arancini

Prep time: 5 minutes | Cook time: 8 to 11 minutes | Makes 16 arancini

250 g cooked rice, cooled	2 tablespoons minced fresh basil
2 eggs, beaten	
90 g panko breadcrumbs, divided	16 ¾-inch cubes mozzarella cheese cheese
45 g grated Parmesan cheese	2 tablespoons olive oil

1. Preheat the air fryer to 200°C. 2. In a medium-sized bowl, combine the rice, eggs, 120 ml of the breadcrumbs, Parmesan cheese, and basil. Form this mixture into 16 1½-inch balls. 3. Poke a hole in each of the balls with your finger and insert a mozzarella cheese cube. Form the rice mixture firmly around the cheese. 4. On a shallow plate, combine the remaining 100 g of the breadcrumbs with the olive oil and mix well. Roll the rice balls in the breadcrumbs to coat. 5. Air fry the arancini in batches for 8 to 11 minutes or until golden. 6. Serve hot.

Pepperoni Pizza Dip

Prep time: 10 minutes | Cook time: 10 minutes | Serves 6

170 g soft white cheese	pepperoni
85 g shredded Italian cheese blend	400 g sliced black olives
60 ml soured cream	1 tablespoon thinly sliced spring onion
1½ teaspoons dried Italian seasoning	Cut-up raw mixed vegetables, toasted baguette slices, pitta chips, or tortilla chips, for serving
¼ teaspoon garlic salt	
¼ teaspoon onion powder	
165 g pizza sauce	
42 g sliced miniature	

1. In a small bowl, combine the soft white cheese, 28 g of the shredded cheese, the soured cream, Italian seasoning, garlic salt, and onion powder. Stir until smooth and the ingredients are well blended. 2. Spread the mixture in a baking pan. Top with the pizza sauce, spreading to the edges. Sprinkle with the remaining 56 g shredded cheese. Arrange the pepperoni slices on top of the cheese. Top with the black olives and green onion. 3. Place the pan in the air fryer basket. Set the air fryer to 180°C for 10 minutes, or until the pepperoni is beginning to brown on the edges and the cheese is bubbly and lightly browned. 4. Let stand for 5 minutes before serving with mixed vegetables, toasted baguette slices, pitta chips, or tortilla chips.

Cheese-Stuffed Blooming Onion

Prep time: 10 minutes | Cook time: 15 minutes | Serves 2

1 large brown onion (397 g)	3 tablespoons mayonnaise
1 tablespoon olive oil	1 tablespoon fresh lemon juice
Rock salt and freshly ground black pepper, to taste	1 tablespoon chopped fresh flat-leaf parsley parsley
18 g plus 2 tablespoons panko breadcrumbs	2 teaspoons wholemeal Dijon mustard
22 g grated Parmesan cheese	1 garlic clove, minced

1. Place the onion on a cutting board and trim the top off and peel off the outer skin. Turn the onion upside down and use a paring knife, cut vertical slits halfway through the onion at ½-inch intervals around the onion, keeping the root intact. When you turn the onion right side up, it should open up like the petals of a flower. Drizzle the cut sides of the onion with the olive oil and season with salt and pepper. Place petal-side up in the air fryer and air fry at 180°C for 10 minutes. 2. Meanwhile, in a bowl, stir together the panko, Parmesan, mayonnaise, lemon juice, parsley, mustard, and garlic until incorporated into a smooth paste. 3. Remove the onion from the fryer and stuff the paste all over and in between the onion "petals." Return the onion to the air fryer and air fry at 190°C until the onion is tender in the centre and the bread crumb mixture is golden, about 5 minutes. Remove the onion from the air fryer, transfer to a plate, and serve hot.

Lebanese Muhammara

Prep time: 15 minutes | Cook time: 15 minutes | Serves 6

2 large red peppers	1 teaspoon rock salt
60 ml plus 2 tablespoons extra-virgin olive oil	1 teaspoon red pepper flakes
85 g walnut halves	Raw mixed vegetables (such as cucumber, carrots, sliced courgette, or cauliflower) or toasted pitta bread chips, for serving
1 tablespoon agave syrup or honey	
1 teaspoon fresh lemon juice	
1 teaspoon cumin powder	

1. Drizzle the peppers with 2 tablespoons of the olive oil and place in the air fryer basket. Set the air fryer to 200°C for 10 minutes. 2. Add the walnuts to the basket, arranging them around the peppers. Set the air fryer to 200°C for 5 minutes. 3. Remove the peppers, seal in a a resealable plastic bag, and let rest for 5 to 10 minutes. Transfer the walnuts to a plate and set aside to cool down. 4. Place the softened peppers, walnuts, agave, lemon juice, cumin, salt, and ½ teaspoon of the pepper flakes blend in a food processor until smooth. 5. Transfer the dip to a serving bowl and create an indentation in the middle. Pour the remaining 60 ml olive oil into the indentation. Garnish the dip with the remaining ½ teaspoon pepper flakes. 6. Serve with mixed vegetables or toasted pitta bread chips.

Sea Salt Potato Crisps

Prep time: 30 minutes | Cook time: 27 minutes | Serves 4

Oil, for spraying	1 tablespoon oil
4 medium-sized yellow potatoes such as Maris Piper potatoes	⅛ to ¼ teaspoon fine sea salt

1. Line the air fryer basket with baking paper and spray lightly with oil. 2. Using a mandoline or a very sharp knife, cut the potatoes into very thin slices. 3. Place the slices in a bowl of cold water and let soak for about 20 minutes. 4. Drain the potatoes, transfer them to a plate lined with kitchen roll, and pat dry. 5. Drizzle the oil over the potatoes, sprinkle with the salt, and toss to combine. Transfer to the prepared basket. 6. Air fry at 90°C for 20 minutes. Toss the crisps, increase the heat to 200°C, and cook for another 5 to 7 minutes, until crispy.

Peppery Chicken Meatballs

Prep time: 5 minutes | Cook time: 13 to 20 minutes | Makes 16 meatballs

2 teaspoons olive oil	1 egg white
35 g minced onion	½ teaspoon dried thyme
35 g minced red pepper	230 g minced chicken breast
2 vanilla wafers, crushed	

1. Preheat the air fryer to 188°C. 2. In a baking pan, mix the olive oil, onion, and red pepper. Put the pan in the air fryer. Air fry for 3 to 5 minutes, or until the mixed vegetables are tender. 3. In a medium-sized bowl, mix the cooked mixed vegetables, crushed wafers, egg white, and thyme until well combined 4. Mix in the chicken, gently but thoroughly, until everything is combined. 5. Form the mixture into 16 meatballs and place them in the air fryer basket. Air fry for 10 to 15 minutes, or until the meatballs reach an internal temperature of 70°C on a meat thermometer. 6. Serve immediately.

Roasted Grape Dip

Prep time: 10 minutes | Cook time: 8 to 12 minutes | Serves 6

475 g seedless red grapes, rinsed and patted dry	yoghurt
1 tablespoon apple cider vinegar	2 tablespoons semi-skimmed milk
1 tablespoon honey	2 tablespoons minced fresh basil
240 ml low-fat Greek	

1. In the air fryer basket, sprinkle the grapes with the cider vinegar and drizzle with the honey. Toss to coat. Roast the grapes at 190°C for 8 to 12 minutes, or until shrivelled but still soft. Remove from the air fryer. 2. In a medium-sized bowl, stir together the yoghurt and milk. 3. Gently blend in the grapes and basil. Serve immediately or cover and chill for 1 to 2 hours.

Onion Pakoras

Prep time: 30 minutes | Cook time: 10 minutes per batch | Serves 2

two medium-sized brown or white onions, sliced (475 g)	2 tablespoons gram flour
	1 teaspoon turmeric powder
30 g finely chopped fresh coriander	1 teaspoon cumin seeds
	1 teaspoon rock salt
2 tablespoons mixed vegetables oil	½ teaspoon cayenne pepper
1 tablespoon gram flour	mixed vegetables oil spray
1 tablespoon rice flour, or	

1. 1.In a large bowl, combine the onions, coriander, oil, gram flour, rice flour, turmeric, cumin seeds, salt, and cayenne. Stir to combine. Cover and let stand for 30 minutes or up to overnight. (This allows the onions to release moisture, creating a batter.) Mix well before using. 2. Spray the air fryer basket generously with mixed vegetables oil spray. Drop half of the batter in 6 heaped tablespoons into the basket. Set the air fryer to 180ºC for 8 minutes. Carefully turn the pakoras over and spray with oil spray. Set the air fryer for 2 minutes, or until the batter is fully cooked and crisp. 3. Repeat with remaining batter to make 6 more pakoras, checking at 6 minutes for degree of doneness. Serve hot.

Bacon-Wrapped Prawns and Jalapeño Chillies

Prep time: 20 minutes | Cook time: 26 minutes | Serves 8

24 large prawns, peeled and deveined, about 340 g	12 strips bacon, cut in half
5 tablespoons barbecue sauce, divided	24 small pickled jalapeño chillies slices

1. Toss together the prawns and 3 tablespoons of the barbecue sauce. Let stand for 15 minutes. Soak 24 wooden cocktail sticks in water for 10 minutes. Wrap 1 piece bacon around the prawns and jalapeño chillies slice, then secure with a cocktail stick. 2. Preheat the air fryer to 180ºC. 3. Working in batches, place half of the prawns in the air fryer basket, spacing them ½ inch apart. Air fry for 10 minutes. Turn prawns over with tongs and air fry for 3 minutes more, or until bacon is golden and prawns are fully cooked. 4. Brush with the remaining barbecue sauce and serve.

Homemade Sweet Potato Chips

Prep time: 5 minutes | Cook time: 15 minutes | Serves 2

1 large sweet potato, sliced thin	⅛ teaspoon salt
	2 tablespoons olive oil

1. Preheat the air fryer to 190ºC. 2. In a small bowl, toss the sweet potatoes, salt, and olive oil together until the potatoes are well coated. 3. Put the sweet potato slices into the air fryer and spread them out in a single layer. 4. Fry for 10 minutes. Stir, then air fry for 3 to 5 minutes more, or until the chips reach the preferred level of crispiness.

Veggie Salmon Nachos

Prep time: 10 minutes | Cook time: 9 to 12 minutes | Serves 6

57 g baked no-salt sweetcorn tortilla chips	1 red pepper, chopped
	50 g grated carrot
1 (142 g) baked salmon fillet, flaked	1 jalapeño chillies pepper, minced
100 g canned low-salt black beans, rinsed and drained	30 g shredded low-salt low-fat Swiss cheese
	1 tomato, chopped

1. Preheat the air fryer to 180ºC. 2. In a baking pan, layer the tortilla chips. Top with the salmon, black beans, red pepper, carrot, jalapeño chillies, and Swiss cheese. 3. Bake in the air fryer for 9 to 12 minutes, or until the cheese is melted and starts to brown. 4. Top with the tomato and serve.

Spicy Chicken Bites

Prep time: 10 minutes | Cook time: 10 to 12 minutes | Makes 30 bites

227 g boneless and skinless chicken thighs, cut into 30 pieces	¼ teaspoon rock salt
	2 tablespoons hot sauce
	Cooking spray

1. Preheat the air fryer to 200ºC. 2. Spray the air fryer basket with cooking spray and season the chicken bites with the rock salt, then place in the basket and air fry for 10 to 12 minutes or until crispy. 3. While the chicken bites cook, pour the hot sauce into a large bowl. 4. Remove the bites and add to the sauce bowl, tossing to coat. Serve warm.

Classic Spring Rolls

Prep time: 10 minutes | Cook time: 9 minutes | Makes 16 spring rolls

4 teaspoons toasted sesame oil	80 g grated carrot
6 medium garlic cloves, minced or pressed	½ teaspoon sea salt
	16 rice paper wrappers
1 tablespoon grated peeled fresh ginger	Cooking oil spray (sunflower, safflower, or refined coconut)
70 g thinly sliced shiitake mushrooms	Gluten-free sweet and sour sauce or Thai sweet chilli sauce, for serving (optional)
500 g chopped green cabbage	

1. Place a wok or sauté pan over medium heat until hot. 2. Add the sesame oil, garlic, ginger, mushrooms, cabbage, carrot, and salt. Cook for 3 to 4 minutes, stirring often, until the cabbage is lightly wilted. Remove the pan from the heat. 3. Gently run a rice paper under water. Lay it on a flat non-absorbent surface. Place about 30 g of the cabbage filling in the middle. Once the wrapper is soft enough to roll, fold the bottom up over the filling, fold in the sides, and roll the wrapper all the way up. (Basically, make a tiny burrito.) 4. Repeat step 3 to make the remaining spring rolls until you have the number of spring rolls you want to cook right now (and the amount that will fit in the air fryer basket in a single layer without them touching each other). Refrigerate any leftover filling in an airtight container for about 1 week. 5. Insert the crisper plate into the basket and the basket into the unit. Preheat the unit by selecting AIR FRY, setting the temperature to 200ºC, and setting the time to 3 minutes. Select START/STOP to begin. 6. Once the unit is preheated, spray the crisper plate and the basket with cooking oil. Place the spring rolls into the basket, leaving a little room between them so they don't stick to each other. Spray the top of each spring roll with cooking oil. 7. Select AIR FRY, set the temperature to 200ºC, and set the time to 9 minutes. Select START/STOP to begin. 8. When the cooking is complete, the egg rolls should be crisp-ish and lightly browned. Serve immediately, plain or with a sauce of choice.

Rosemary-Garlic Shoestring Fries

Prep time: 5 minutes | Cook time: 18 minutes | Serves 2

1 large russet potatoes or Maris Piper potato (about 340 g), scrubbed clean, and julienned	rosemary
	Rock salt and freshly ground black pepper, to taste
1 tablespoon mixed vegetables oil	1 garlic clove, thinly sliced
Leaves from 1 sprig fresh	Flaky sea salt, for serving

1. Preheat the air fryer to 200ºC. 2. Place the julienned potatoes in a large colander and rinse under cold running water until the water runs clear. Spread the potatoes out on a double layer of kitchen roll and pat dry. 3. In a large bowl, combine the potatoes, oil, and rosemary. Season with rock salt and pepper and toss to coat evenly. Place the potatoes in the air fryer and air fry for 18 minutes, shaking the basket every 5 minutes and adding the garlic in the last 5 minutes of cooking, or until the fries are golden and crisp. 4. Transfer the fries to a plate and sprinkle with flaky sea salt while they're hot. Serve immediately.

Air Fried Pot Stickers

Prep time: 10 minutes | Cook time: 18 to 20 minutes | Makes 30 pot stickers

35 g finely chopped cabbage	2 tablespoons cocktail sauce
30 g finely chopped red pepper	2 teaspoons low-salt soy sauce
2 spring onions, finely chopped	30 wonton wrappers
1 egg, beaten	1 tablespoon water, for brushing the wrappers

1. Preheat the air fryer to 180°C. 2. In a small bowl, combine the cabbage, pepper, spring onions, egg, cocktail sauce, and soy sauce, and mix well. 3. Put about 1 teaspoon of the mixture in the centre of each wonton wrapper. Fold the wrapper in half, covering the filling; dampen the edges with water, and seal. You can crimp the edges of the wrapper with your fingers, so they look like the pot stickers you get in restaurants. Brush them with water. 4. Place the pot stickers in the air fryer basket and air fry in 2 batches for 9 to 10 minutes, or until the pot stickers are hot and the bottoms are lightly browned. 5. Serve hot.

Crispy Filo Artichoke Triangles

Prep time: 15 minutes | Cook time: 9 to 12 minutes | Makes 18 triangles

70 g Ricotta cheese	½ teaspoon dried thyme
1 egg white	6 sheets frozen filo pastry, thawed
60 g minced and drained artichoke hearts	2 tablespoons melted butter
3 tablespoons grated mozzarella cheese cheese	

1. Preheat the air fryer to 200°C. 2. In a small bowl, combine the Ricotta cheese, egg white, artichoke hearts, mozzarella cheese cheese, and thyme, and mix well. 3. Cover the filo pastry with a damp kitchen towel while you work so it doesn't dry out. Using one sheet at a time, place on the work surface and cut into thirds lengthwise. 4. Put about 1½ teaspoons of the filling on each strip at the base. Fold the bottom right-hand tip of phyllo over the filling to meet the other side in a triangle, then continue folding in a triangle. Brush each triangle with butter to seal the edges. Repeat with the remaining phyllo dough and filling. 5. Place the triangles in the air fryer basket. Bake, 6 at a time, for about 3 to 4 minutes, or until the filo is golden and crisp. 6. Serve hot.

Courgette Feta Roulades

Prep time: 10 minutes | Cook time: 10 minutes | Serves 6

55 g feta cheese	⅛ teaspoon salt
1 garlic clove, minced	⅛ teaspoon red pepper flakes
2 tablespoons fresh basil, minced	1 tablespoon lemon juice
1 tablespoon capers, minced	2 medium courgette
	12 cocktail sticks

1. Preheat the air fryer to 180°C. (If using a grill attachment, make sure it is inside the air fryer during preheating.) 2. In a small bowl, combine the feta cheese, garlic, basil, capers, salt, red pepper flakes, and lemon juice. 3. Slice the courgette into ⅛-inch strips lengthwise. (Each courgette should yield around 6 strips.) 4. Spread 1 tablespoon of the cheese filling onto each slice of courgette, then roll it up and secure it with a cocktail stick through the middle. 5. Place the courgette roulades into the air fryer basket in a single layer, making sure that they don't touch each other. 6. Bake or grill in the air fryer for 10 minutes. 7. Remove the courgette roulades from the air fryer and gently remove the cocktail sticks before serving.

Rumaki

Prep time: 30 minutes | Cook time: 10 to 12 minutes per batch | Makes about 24 rumaki

283 g raw chicken livers	60 ml low-salt teriyaki sauce
1 can sliced water chestnuts, drained	12 slices turkey bacon

Snacks and Appetizers

1. Cut livers into 1½-inch pieces, trimming out tough veins as you slice. 2. Place livers, water chestnuts, and teriyaki sauce in small container with lid. If needed, add another tablespoon of teriyaki sauce to make sure livers are covered. Refrigerate for 1 hour. 3. When ready to cook, cut bacon slices in half crosswise. 4. Wrap 1 piece of liver and 1 slice of water chestnut in each bacon strip. Secure with a cocktail stick. 5. When you have wrapped half of the livers, place them in the air fryer basket in a single layer. 6. Air fry at 200ºC for 10 to 12 minutes, until liver is done, and bacon is crispy. 7. While first batch cooks, wrap the remaining livers. Repeat step 6 to cook your second batch.

Chapter 8
Vegetables and Sides

Courgette Fritters

Prep time: 10 minutes | Cook time: 10 minutes | Serves 4

2 courgette, grated (about 450 g)	¼ teaspoon ground turmeric
1 teaspoon salt	¼ teaspoon freshly ground black pepper
25 g almond flour	1 tablespoon olive oil
20 g grated Parmesan cheese	½ lemon, sliced into wedges
1 large egg	
¼ teaspoon dried thyme	

1. Preheat the air fryer to 200°C. Cut a piece of parchment paper to fit slightly smaller than the bottom of the air fryer. 2. Place the courgette in a large colander and sprinkle with the salt. Let sit for 5 to 10 minutes. Squeeze as much liquid as you can from the courgette and place in a large mixing bowl. Add the almond flour, Parmesan, egg, thyme, turmeric, and black pepper. Stir gently until thoroughly combined. 3. Shape the mixture into 8 patties and arrange on the parchment paper. Brush lightly with the olive oil. Pausing halfway through the cooking time to turn the patties, air fry for 10 minutes until golden brown. Serve warm with the lemon wedges.

Southwestern Roasted Corn

Prep time: 10 minutes | Cook time: 10 minutes | Serves 4

Corn:

240 g thawed frozen corn kernels	1 tablespoon fresh lemon juice
50 g diced yellow onion	1 teaspoon ground cumin
150 g mixed diced bell peppers	½ teaspoon ancho chili powder
1 jalapeño, diced	½ teaspoon coarse sea salt

For Serving:

150 g queso fresco or feta cheese	coriander
10 g chopped fresh	1 tablespoon fresh lemon juice

1. For the corn: In a large bowl, stir together the corn, onion, bell peppers, jalapeño, lemon juice, cumin, chili powder, and salt until well incorporated. 2. Pour the spiced vegetables into the air fryer basket. Set the air fryer to 190°C for 10 minutes, stirring halfway through the cooking time. 3. Transfer the corn mixture to a serving bowl. Add the cheese, coriander, and lemon juice and stir well to combine. Serve immediately.

Garlic Courgette and Red Peppers

Prep time: 5 minutes | Cook time: 15 minutes | Serves 6

2 medium courgette, cubed	2 garlic cloves, sliced
1 red pepper, diced	2 tablespoons olive oil
	½ teaspoon salt

1. Preheat the air fryer to 193°C. 2. In a large bowl, mix together the courgette, bell pepper, and garlic with the olive oil and salt. 3. Pour the mixture into the air fryer basket, and roast for 7 minutes. Shake or stir, then roast for 7 to 8 minutes more.

Mexican Corn in a Cup

Prep time: 5 minutes | Cook time: 10 minutes | Serves 4

650 g frozen corn kernels (do not thaw)	queso fresco)
Vegetable oil spray	2 tablespoons fresh lemon or lime juice
2 tablespoons butter	1 teaspoon chili powder
60 g sour cream	Chopped fresh green onion (optional)
60 g mayonnaise	Chopped fresh coriander (optional)
20 g grated Parmesan cheese (or feta, cotija, or	

1. Place the corn in the bottom of the air fryer basket and spray with vegetable oil spray. Set the air fryer to 180°C for 10 minutes. 2. Transfer the corn to a serving bowl. Add the butter and stir until melted. Add the sour cream, mayonnaise, cheese, lemon juice, and chili powder; stir until well combined. Serve immediately with green onion and coriander (if using).

Parmesan-Thyme Butternut Squash

Prep time: 15 minutes | Cook time: 20 minutes | Serves 4

350 g butternut squash, cubed into 1-inch pieces (approximately 1 medium)	¼ teaspoon salt
	¼ teaspoon garlic powder
	¼ teaspoon black pepper
	1 tablespoon fresh thyme
2 tablespoons olive oil	20 g grated Parmesan

1. Preheat the air fryer to 180°C. 2. In a large bowl, combine the cubed squash with the olive oil, salt, garlic powder, pepper, and thyme until the squash is well coated. 3. Pour this mixture into the air fryer basket, and roast for 10 minutes. Stir and roast another 8 to 10 minutes more. 4. Remove the squash from the air fryer and toss with freshly grated Parmesan before serving.

Parsnip Fries with Romesco Sauce

Prep time: 20 minutes | Cook time: 24 minutes | Serves 4

Romesco Sauce:

1 red pepper, halved and seeded	and seeded
	1 tablespoon red wine vinegar
1 (1-inch) thick slice of Italian bread, torn into pieces	¼ teaspoon smoked paprika
130 g almonds, toasted	½ teaspoon salt
Olive oil	180 ml olive oil
½ Jalapeño pepper, seeded	3 parsnips, peeled and cut into long strips
1 tablespoon fresh parsley leaves	2 teaspoons olive oil
1 clove garlic	Salt and freshly ground black pepper, to taste
2 plum tomatoes, peeled	

1. Preheat the air fryer to 200°C. 2. Place the red pepper halves, cut side down, in the air fryer basket and air fry for 8 to 10 minutes, or until the skin turns black all over. Remove the pepper from the air fryer and let it cool. When it is cool enough to handle, peel the pepper. 3. Toss the torn bread and almonds with a little olive oil and air fry for 4 minutes, shaking the basket a couple times throughout the cooking time. When the bread and almonds are nicely toasted, remove them from the air fryer and let them cool for just a minute or two. 4. Combine the toasted bread, almonds, roasted red pepper, Jalapeño pepper, parsley, garlic, tomatoes, vinegar, smoked paprika and salt in a food processor or blender. Process until smooth. With the processor running, add the olive oil through the feed tube until the sauce comes together in a smooth paste that is barely pourable. 5. Toss the parsnip strips with the olive oil, salt and freshly ground black pepper and air fry at 200°C for 10 minutes, shaking the basket a couple times during the cooking process so they brown and cook evenly. Serve the parsnip fries warm with the Romesco sauce to dip into.

Mashed Sweet Potato Tots

Prep time: 10 minutes | Cook time: 12 to 13 minutes per batch | Makes 18 to 24 tots

210 g cooked mashed sweet potatoes	pecans
	1½ teaspoons honey
1 egg white, beaten	Salt, to taste
⅛ teaspoon ground cinnamon	50 g panko bread crumbs
	Oil for misting or cooking spray
1 dash nutmeg	
2 tablespoons chopped	

1. Preheat the air fryer to 200°C. 2. In a large bowl, mix together the potatoes, egg white, cinnamon, nutmeg, pecans, honey, and salt to taste. 3. Place panko crumbs on a sheet of wax paper. 4. For each tot, use about 2 teaspoons of sweet potato mixture. To shape, drop the measure of potato mixture onto panko crumbs and push crumbs up and around potatoes to coat edges. Then turn tot over to coat other side with crumbs. 5. Mist tots with oil or cooking spray and place in air fryer basket in single layer. 6. Air fry at 200°C for 12 to 13 minutes, until browned and crispy. 7. Repeat steps 5 and 6 to cook remaining tots.

Sweet and Crispy Roasted Pearl Onions

Prep time: 5 minutes | Cook time: 18 minutes | Serves 3

1 (410 g) package frozen pearl onions (do not thaw)	vinegar
	2 teaspoons finely chopped fresh rosemary
2 tablespoons extra-virgin olive oil	½ teaspoon coarse sea salt
	¼ teaspoon black pepper
2 tablespoons balsamic	

1. In a medium bowl, combine the onions, olive oil, vinegar, rosemary, salt, and pepper until well coated. 2. Transfer the onions to the air fryer basket. Set the air fryer to 200ºC for 18 minutes, or until the onions are tender and lightly charred, stirring once or twice during the cooking time.

Garlic-Parmesan Crispy Baby Potatoes

Prep time: 10 minutes | Cook time: 15 minutes | Serves 4

Oil, for spraying	½ teaspoon salt
450 g baby potatoes	¼ teaspoon freshly ground black pepper
45 g grated Parmesan cheese, divided	¼ teaspoon paprika
3 tablespoons olive oil	2 tablespoons chopped fresh parsley, for garnish
2 teaspoons garlic powder	
½ teaspoon onion powder	

1. Line the air fryer basket with parchment and spray lightly with oil. 2. Rinse the potatoes, pat dry with paper towels, and place in a large bowl. 3. In a small bowl, mix together 45 g of Parmesan cheese, the olive oil, garlic, onion powder, salt, black pepper, and paprika. Pour the mixture over the potatoes and toss to coat. 4. Transfer the potatoes to the prepared basket and spread them out in an even layer, taking care to keep them from touching. You may need to work in batches, depending on the size of your air fryer. 5. Air fry at 200ºC for 15 minutes, stirring after 7 to 8 minutes, or until easily pierced with a fork.

Continue to cook for another 1 to 2 minutes, if needed. 6. Sprinkle with the parsley and the remaining Parmesan cheese and serve.

Maple-Roasted Tomatoes

Prep time: 15 minutes | Cook time: 20 minutes | Serves 2

280 g cherry tomatoes, halved	2 sprigs fresh thyme, stems removed
coarse sea salt, to taste	1 garlic clove, minced
2 tablespoons maple syrup	Freshly ground black pepper
1 tablespoon vegetable oil	

1. Place the tomatoes in a colander and sprinkle liberally with salt. Let stand for 10 minutes to drain. 2. Transfer the tomatoes cut-side up to a cake pan, then drizzle with the maple syrup, followed by the oil. Sprinkle with the thyme leaves and garlic and season with pepper. Place the pan in the air fryer and roast at 160ºC until the tomatoes are soft, collapsed, and lightly caramelized on top, about 20 minutes. 3. Serve straight from the pan or transfer the tomatoes to a plate and drizzle with the juices from the pan to serve.

Corn Croquettes

Prep time: 10 minutes | Cook time: 12 to 14 minutes | Serves 4

105 g leftover mashed potatoes	⅛ teaspoon ground black pepper
340 g corn kernels (if frozen, thawed, and well drained)	¼ teaspoon salt
	50 g panko bread crumbs
	Oil for misting or cooking spray
¼ teaspoon onion powder	

1. Place the potatoes and half the corn in food processor and pulse until corn is well chopped. 2. Transfer mixture to large bowl and stir in remaining corn, onion powder, pepper and salt. 3. Shape mixture into 16 balls. 4. Roll balls in panko crumbs, mist with oil or cooking spray, and place in air fryer basket. 5. Air fry at 180ºC for 12 to 14 minutes, until golden brown and crispy.

Sausage-Stuffed Mushroom Caps

Prep time: 10 minutes | Cook time: 8 minutes | Serves 2

6 large portobello mushroom caps	flour
230 g Italian sausage	20 g grated Parmesan cheese
15 g chopped onion	1 teaspoon minced fresh garlic
2 tablespoons blanched finely ground almond	

1. Use a spoon to hollow out each mushroom cap, reserving scrapings. 2. In a medium skillet over medium heat, brown the sausage about 10 minutes or until fully cooked and no pink remains. Drain and then add reserved mushroom scrapings, onion, almond flour, Parmesan, and garlic. Gently fold ingredients together and continue cooking an additional minute, then remove from heat. 3. Evenly spoon the mixture into mushroom caps and place the caps into a 6-inch round pan. Place pan into the air fryer basket. 4. Adjust the temperature to 190ºC and set the timer for 8 minutes. 5. When finished cooking, the tops will be browned and bubbling. Serve warm.

Butter and Garlic Fried Cabbage

Prep time: 5 minutes | Cook time: 9 minutes | Serves 2

Oil, for spraying	1 teaspoon granulated garlic
½ head cabbage, cut into bite-size pieces	½ teaspoon coarse sea salt
2 tablespoons unsalted butter, melted	¼ teaspoon freshly ground black pepper

1. Line the air fryer basket with parchment and spray lightly with oil. 2. In a large bowl, mix together the cabbage, butter, garlic, salt, and black pepper until evenly coated. 3. Transfer the cabbage to the prepared basket and spray lightly with oil. 4. Air fry at 190ºC for 5 minutes, toss, and cook for another 3 to 4 minutes, or until lightly crispy.

Crispy Lemon Artichoke Hearts

Prep time: 10 minutes | Cook time: 15 minutes | Serves 2

1 (425 g) can artichoke hearts in water, drained	crumbs
1 egg	¼ teaspoon salt
1 tablespoon water	¼ teaspoon paprika
30 g whole wheat bread	½ lemon

1. Preheat the air fryer to 190ºC. 2. In a medium shallow bowl, beat together the egg and water until frothy. 3. In a separate medium shallow bowl, mix together the bread crumbs, salt, and paprika. 4. Dip each artichoke heart into the egg mixture, then into the bread crumb mixture, coating the outside with the crumbs. Place the artichokes hearts in a single layer of the air fryer basket. 5. Fry the artichoke hearts for 15 minutes. 6. Remove the artichokes from the air fryer, and squeeze fresh lemon juice over the top before serving.

Tofu Bites

Prep time: 15 minutes | Cook time: 30 minutes | Serves 4

1 packaged firm tofu, cubed and pressed to remove excess water	1 teaspoon hot sauce
	2 tablespoons sesame seeds
1 tablespoon soy sauce	1 teaspoon garlic powder
1 tablespoon ketchup	Salt and ground black pepper, to taste
1 tablespoon maple syrup	Cooking spray
½ teaspoon vinegar	
1 teaspoon liquid smoke	

1. Preheat the air fryer to 190ºC. 2. Spritz a baking dish with cooking spray. 3. Combine all the ingredients to coat the tofu completely and allow the marinade to absorb for half an hour. 4. Transfer the tofu to the baking dish, then air fry for 15 minutes. Flip the tofu over and air fry for another 15 minutes on the other side. 5. Serve immediately.

Gold Artichoke Hearts

Prep time: 15 minutes | Cook time: 8 minutes | Serves 4

12 whole artichoke hearts packed in water, drained	40 g panko bread crumbs
60 g plain flour	1 teaspoon Italian seasoning
1 egg	Cooking oil spray

1. Squeeze any excess water from the artichoke hearts and place them on paper towels to dry. 2. Place the flour in a small bowl. 3. In another small bowl, beat the egg. 4. In a third small bowl, stir together the panko and Italian seasoning. 5. Dip the artichoke hearts in the flour, in the egg, and into the panko mixture until coated. 6. Insert the crisper plate into the basket and the basket into the unit. Preheat the unit by selecting AIR FRY, setting the temperature to 190ºC, and setting the time to 3 minutes. Select START/STOP to begin. 7. Once the unit is preheated, spray the crisper plate and the basket with cooking oil. Place the breaded artichoke hearts into the basket, stacking them if needed. 8. Select AIR FRY, set the temperature to 190ºC, and set the time to 8 minutes. Select START/STOP to begin. 9. After 4 minutes, use tongs to flip the artichoke hearts. I recommend flipping instead of shaking because the hearts are small, and this will help keep the breading intact. Re-insert the basket to resume cooking. 10. When the cooking is complete, the artichoke hearts should be deep golden brown and crisp. Cool for 5 minutes before serving.

Turnip Fries

Prep time: 10 minutes | Cook time: 20 to 30 minutes | Serves 4

900 g turnip, peeled and cut into ¼ to ½-inch fries	Salt and freshly ground black pepper, to taste
2 tablespoons olive oil	

1. Preheat the air fryer to 200ºC. 2. In a large bowl, combine the turnip and olive oil. Season to taste with salt and black pepper. Toss gently until thoroughly coated. 3. Working in batches if necessary, spread the turnip in a single layer in the air fryer basket. Pausing halfway through the cooking time to shake the basket, air fry for 20 to 30 minutes until the fries are lightly browned and crunchy.

Glazed Sweet Potato Bites

Prep time: 10 minutes | Cook time: 25 minutes | Serves 4

Oil, for spraying	2 tablespoons honey
3 medium sweet potatoes, peeled and cut into 1-inch pieces	1 tablespoon olive oil
	2 teaspoons ground cinnamon

1. Line the air fryer basket with parchment and spray lightly with oil. 2. In a large bowl, toss together the sweet potatoes, honey, olive oil, and cinnamon until evenly coated. 3. Place the potatoes in the prepared basket. 4. Air fry at 200ºC for 20 to 25 minutes, or until crispy and easily pierced with a fork.

Asian-Inspired Roasted Broccoli

Prep time: 10 minutes | Cook time: 15 minutes | Serves 4

Broccoli:

Oil, for spraying	1 tablespoon minced garlic
450 g broccoli florets	½ teaspoon salt
2 teaspoons peanut oil	

Sauce:

2 tablespoons soy sauce	2 teaspoons Sriracha
2 teaspoons honey	1 teaspoon rice vinegar

Make the Broccoli 1. Line the air fryer basket with parchment and spray lightly with oil. 2. In a large bowl, toss together the broccoli, peanut oil, garlic, and salt until evenly coated. 3. Spread out the broccoli in an even layer in the prepared basket. 4. Air fry at 200ºC for 15 minutes, stirring halfway through. Make the Sauce 5. Meanwhile, in a small microwave-safe bowl, combine the soy sauce, honey, Sriracha, and rice vinegar and microwave on high for about 15 seconds. Stir to combine. 6. Transfer the broccoli to a serving bowl and add the sauce. Gently toss until evenly coated and serve immediately.

Fried Asparagus

Prep time: 5 minutes | Cook time: 12 minutes | Serves 4

1 tablespoon olive oil	¼ teaspoon ground black pepper
450 g asparagus spears, ends trimmed	1 tablespoon salted butter, melted
¼ teaspoon salt	

1. In a large bowl, drizzle olive oil over asparagus spears and sprinkle with salt and pepper. 2. Place spears into ungreased air fryer basket. Adjust the temperature to 190°C and set the timer for 12 minutes, shaking the basket halfway through cooking. Asparagus will be lightly browned and tender when done. 3. Transfer to a large dish and drizzle with butter. Serve warm.

Fried Brussels Sprouts

Prep time: 10 minutes | Cook time: 18 minutes | Serves 4

1 teaspoon plus 1 tablespoon extra-virgin olive oil, divided	2 tablespoons sriracha
2 teaspoons minced garlic	450 g Brussels sprouts, stems trimmed and any tough leaves removed, rinsed, halved lengthwise, and dried
2 tablespoons honey	
1 tablespoon sugar	
2 tablespoons freshly squeezed lemon juice	½ teaspoon salt
2 tablespoons rice vinegar	Cooking oil spray

1. In a small saucepan over low heat, combine 1 teaspoon of olive oil, the garlic, honey, sugar, lemon juice, vinegar, and sriracha. Cook for 2 to 3 minutes, or until slightly thickened. Remove the pan from the heat, cover, and set aside. 2. Place the Brussels sprouts in a resealable bag or small bowl. Add the remaining olive oil and the salt, and toss to coat. 3. Insert the crisper plate into the basket and the basket into the unit. Preheat the unit by selecting AIR FRY, setting the temperature to 200°C, and setting the time to 3 minutes. Select START/STOP to begin. 4. Once the unit is preheated, spray the crisper plate with cooking oil. Add the Brussels sprouts to the basket. 5. Select AIR FRY, set the temperature to 200°C, and set the time to 15 minutes. Select START/STOP to begin. 6. After 7 or 8 minutes, remove the basket and shake it to toss the sprouts. Reinsert the basket to resume cooking. 7. When the cooking is complete, the leaves should be crispy and light brown and the sprout centres tender. 8. Place the sprouts in a medium serving bowl and drizzle the sauce over the top. Toss to coat, and serve immediately.

Crispy Garlic Sliced Aubergine

Prep time: 5 minutes | Cook time: 25 minutes | Serves 4

1 egg	½ teaspoon salt
1 tablespoon water	½ teaspoon paprika
60 g whole wheat bread crumbs	1 medium aubergine, sliced into ¼-inch-thick rounds
1 teaspoon garlic powder	
½ teaspoon dried oregano	1 tablespoon olive oil

1. Preheat the air fryer to 180°C. 2. In a medium shallow bowl, beat together the egg and water until frothy. 3. In a separate medium shallow bowl, mix together bread crumbs, garlic powder, oregano, salt, and paprika. 4. Dip each aubergine slice into the egg mixture, then into the bread crumb mixture, coating the outside with crumbs. Place the slices in a single layer in the bottom of the air fryer basket. 5. Drizzle the tops of the aubergine slices with the olive oil, then fry for 15 minutes. Turn each slice and cook for an additional 10 minutes.

Roasted Aubergine

Prep time: 15 minutes | Cook time: 15 minutes | Serves 4

1 large aubergine	¼ teaspoon salt
2 tablespoons olive oil	½ teaspoon garlic powder

1. Remove top and bottom from aubergine. Slice aubergine into ¼-inch-thick round slices. 2. Brush slices with olive oil. Sprinkle with salt and garlic powder. Place aubergine slices into the air fryer basket. 3. Adjust the temperature to 200°C and set the timer for 15 minutes. 4. Serve immediately.

Garlic and Thyme Tomatoes

Prep time: 10 minutes | Cook time: 15 minutes | Serves 2 to 4

4 plum tomatoes	1 clove garlic, minced
1 tablespoon olive oil	½ teaspoon dried thyme
Salt and freshly ground black pepper, to taste	

1. Preheat the air fryer to 200°C. 2. Cut the tomatoes in half and scoop out the seeds and any pithy parts with your fingers. Place the tomatoes in a bowl and toss with the olive oil, salt, pepper, garlic and thyme. 3. Transfer the tomatoes to the air fryer, cut side up. Air fry for 15 minutes. The edges should just start to brown. Let the tomatoes cool to an edible temperature for a few minutes and then use in pastas, on top of crostini, or as an accompaniment to any poultry, meat or fish.

Indian Aubergine Bharta

Prep time: 15 minutes | Cook time: 20 minutes | Serves 4

1 medium aubergine	2 tablespoons fresh lemon juice
2 tablespoons vegetable oil	2 tablespoons chopped fresh coriander
25 g finely minced onion	½ teaspoon coarse sea salt
100 g finely chopped fresh tomato	⅛ teaspoon cayenne pepper

1. Rub the aubergine all over with the vegetable oil. Place the aubergine in the air fryer basket. Set the air fryer to 200°C for 20 minutes, or until the aubergine skin is blistered and charred. 2. Transfer the aubergine to a re-sealable plastic bag, seal, and set aside for 15 to 20 minutes (the aubergine will finish cooking in the residual heat trapped in the bag). 3. Transfer the aubergine to a large bowl. Peel off and discard the charred skin. Roughly mash the aubergine flesh. Add the onion, tomato, lemon juice, coriander, salt, and cayenne. Stir to combine.

Chapter 9
Vegetarian Mains

Courgette and Spinach Croquettes

Prep time: 9 minutes | Cook time: 7 minutes | Serves 6

4 eggs, slightly beaten	grated
120 g almond flour	⅓ teaspoon red pepper flakes
120 g goat cheese, crumbled	450 g courgette, peeled and grated
1 teaspoon fine sea salt	⅓ teaspoon dried dill weed
4 garlic cloves, minced	
235 g baby spinach	
120 g Parmesan cheese,	

1. Thoroughly combine all ingredients in a bowl. 2. Now, roll the mixture to form small croquettes. 3. Air fry at 170°C for 7 minutes or until golden. 4. Tate, adjust for seasonings and serve warm.

Crispy Aubergine Slices with Parsley

Prep time: 5 minutes | Cook time: 10 to 12 minutes | Serves 4

235 g flour	2 aubergines, sliced
4 eggs	2 garlic cloves, sliced
Salt, to taste	2 tablespoons chopped parsley
475 g breadcrumbs	Cooking spray
1 teaspoon Italian seasoning	

1. Preheat the air fryer to 200°C. 2. Spritz the air fryer basket with cooking spray. 3. On a plate, place the flour. 4. In a shallow bowl, whisk the eggs with salt. 5. In another shallow bowl, combine the breadcrumbs and Italian seasoning. 6. Dredge the aubergine slices, one at a time, in the flour, then in the whisked eggs, finally in the bread crumb mixture to coat well. 7. Arrange the coated aubergine slices in the air fryer basket and air fry for 10 to 12 minutes until golden brown and crispy. 8. Flip the aubergine slices halfway through the cooking time. 9. Transfer the aubergine slices to a plate and sprinkle the garlic and parsley on top before serving.

Italian Baked Egg and Veggies

Prep time: 10 minutes | Cook time: 10 minutes | Serves 2

2 tablespoons salted butter	1 medium plum tomato, diced
1 small courgette, sliced lengthwise and quartered	2 large eggs
½ medium green pepper, seeded and diced	¼ teaspoon onion powder
235 g fresh spinach, chopped	¼ teaspoon garlic powder
	½ teaspoon dried basil
	¼ teaspoon dried oregano

1. Grease two ramekins with 1 tablespoon butter each. 2. In a large bowl, toss courgette, pepper, spinach, and tomato. 3. Divide the mixture in two and place half in each ramekin. 4. Crack an egg on top of each ramekin and sprinkle with onion powder, garlic powder, basil, and oregano. 5. Place into the air fryer basket. 6. Adjust the temperature to 170°C and bake for 10 minutes. 7. Serve immediately.

Black Bean and Tomato Chilli

Prep time: 15 minutes | Cook time: 23 minutes | Serves 6

1 tablespoon olive oil	2 chipotle peppers, chopped
1 medium onion, diced	2 teaspoons cumin
3 garlic cloves, minced	2 teaspoons chilli powder
235 ml vegetable broth	1 teaspoon dried oregano
3 cans black beans, drained and rinsed	½ teaspoon salt
2 cans diced tomatoes	

1. Over a medium heat, fry the garlic and onions in the olive oil for 3 minutes. 2. Add the remaining ingredients, stirring constantly and scraping the bottom to prevent sticking. 3. Preheat the air fryer to 200°C. 4. Take a dish and place the mixture inside. 5. Put a sheet of aluminium foil on top. 6. Transfer to the air fryer and bake for 20 minutes. 7. When ready, plate up and serve immediately.

Vegetarian Mains

Cheesy Cabbage Wedges

Prep time: 5 minutes | Cook time: 20 minutes | Serves 4

4 tablespoons melted butter	cheese
1 head cabbage, cut into wedges	Salt and black pepper, to taste
235 g shredded Parmesan	120 g shredded Mozzarella cheese

1. Preheat the air fryer to 190°C. 2.Brush the melted butter over the cut sides of cabbage wedges and sprinkle both sides with the Parmesan cheese. 3.Season with salt and pepper to taste. 4.Place the cabbage wedges in the air fryer basket and air fry for 20 minutes, flipping the cabbage halfway through, or until the cabbage wedges are lightly browned. 5.Transfer the cabbage wedges to a plate and serve with the Mozzarella cheese sprinkled on top.

Roasted Vegetable Mélange with Herbs

Prep time: 10 minutes | Cook time: 14 to 18 minutes | Serves 4

1 (230 g) package sliced mushrooms	3 cloves garlic, sliced
1 yellow butternut squash, sliced	1 tablespoon olive oil
	½ teaspoon dried basil
1 red pepper, sliced	½ teaspoon dried thyme
	½ teaspoon dried tarragon

1. Preheat the air fryer to 180°C. 2.Toss the mushrooms, squash, and pepper with the garlic and olive oil in a large bowl until well coated. 3.Mix in the basil, thyme, and tarragon and toss again. 4.Spread the vegetables evenly in the air fryer basket and roast for 14 to 18 minutes, or until the vegetables are fork-tender. 5.Cool for 5 minutes before serving.

Loaded Cauliflower Steak

Prep time: 5 minutes | Cook time: 7 minutes | Serves 4

1 medium head cauliflower	60 g blue cheese, crumbled
60 ml hot sauce	60 g full-fat ranch dressing
2 tablespoons salted butter, melted	

1. Remove cauliflower leaves. Slice the head in ½-inch-thick slices. In a small bowl, mix hot sauce and butter. Brush the mixture over the cauliflower. 2.Place each cauliflower steak into the air fryer, working in batches if necessary. 3.Adjust the temperature to 200°C and air fry for 7 minutes. 4.When cooked, edges will begin turning dark and caramelized. To serve, sprinkle steaks with crumbled blue cheese. 5.Drizzle with ranch dressing.

Spinach Cheese Casserole

Prep time: 15 minutes | Cook time: 15 minutes | Serves 4

1 tablespoon salted butter, melted	jalapeños
60 g diced brown onion	475 g fresh spinach, chopped
227 g full fat soft white cheese	475 g cauliflower florets, chopped
80 g full-fat mayonnaise	235 g artichoke hearts, chopped
80 g full-fat sour cream	
60 g chopped pickled	

1. In a large bowl, mix butter, onion, soft white cheese, mayonnaise, and sour cream. 2.Fold in jalapeños, spinach, cauliflower, and artichokes. 3.Pour the mixture into a round baking dish. 4.Cover with foil and place into the air fryer basket. 5.Adjust the temperature to 190°C and set the timer for 15 minutes. 6.In the last 2 minutes of cooking, remove the foil to brown the top. 7.Serve warm.

Cauliflower Rice-Stuffed Peppers

Prep time: 10 minutes | Cook time: 15 minutes | Serves 4

475 g uncooked cauliflower rice	¼ teaspoon salt
180 g drained canned petite diced tomatoes	¼ teaspoon ground black pepper
2 tablespoons olive oil	4 medium green peppers, tops removed, seeded
235 g shredded Mozzarella cheese	

1. In a large bowl, mix all ingredients except peppers. 2.Scoop mixture evenly into peppers. 3.Place peppers into ungreased air fryer basket. 4.Adjust the temperature to 180°C and air fry for 15 minutes. 5.Peppers will be tender, and cheese will be melted when done. 6.Serve warm.

Mediterranean Air Fried Veggies

Prep time: 10 minutes | Cook time: 6 minutes | Serves 4

1 large courgette, sliced	1 teaspoon mixed herbs
235 g cherry tomatoes, halved	1 teaspoon mustard
1 parsnip, sliced	1 teaspoon garlic purée
1 green pepper, sliced	6 tablespoons olive oil
1 carrot, sliced	Salt and ground black pepper, to taste

1. Preheat the air fryer to 200°C. 2.Combine all the ingredients in a bowl, making sure to coat the vegetables well. 3.Transfer to the air fryer and air fry for 6 minutes, ensuring the vegetables are tender and browned. 4.Serve immediately.

Quiche-Stuffed Peppers

Prep time: 5 minutes | Cook time: 15 minutes | Serves 2

2 medium green peppers	60 g diced brown onion
3 large eggs	120 g chopped broccoli
60 g full-fat ricotta cheese	120 g shredded medium Cheddar cheese

1. Cut the tops off of the peppers and remove the seeds and white membranes with a small knife. 2.In a medium bowl, whisk eggs and ricotta. 3.Add onion and broccoli. 4.Pour the egg and vegetable mixture evenly into each pepper. 5.Top with Cheddar. 6.Place peppers into a 1 L round baking dish and place into the air fryer basket. 7.Adjust the temperature to 180°C and bake for 15 minutes. 8.Eggs will be mostly firm and peppers tender when fully cooked. 9.Serve immediately.

Chapter 10

Desserts

Hazelnut Butter Cookies

Prep time: 30 minutes | Cook time: 20 minutes | Serves 10

4 tablespoons liquid monk fruit, or agave syrup	95 g almond flour
	55 g coconut flour
	55 g granulated sweetener
65 g hazelnuts, ground	2 teaspoons ground cinnamon
110 g unsalted butter, room temperature	

1. Firstly, cream liquid monk fruit with butter until the mixture becomes fluffy. Sift in both types of flour. 2. Now, stir in the hazelnuts. Now, knead the mixture to form a dough; place in the refrigerator for about 35 minutes. 3. To finish, shape the prepared dough into the bite-sized balls; arrange them on a baking dish; flatten the balls using the back of a spoon. 4. Mix granulated sweetener with ground cinnamon. Press your cookies in the cinnamon mixture until they are completely covered. 5. Bake the cookies for 20 minutes at 150ºC. 6. Leave them to cool for about 10 minutes before transferring them to a wire rack. Bon appétit !

Double Chocolate Brownies

Prep time: 5 minutes | Cook time: 15 to 20 minutes | Serves 8

55 g almond flour	110 g unsalted butter, melted and cooled
25 g unsweetened cocoa powder	
	3 eggs
½ teaspoon baking powder	1 teaspoon vanilla extract
20 g powdered sweetener	2 tablespoons mini semisweet chocolate chips
¼ teaspoon salt	

1. Preheat the air fryer to 180ºC. Line a cake pan with baking paper and brush with oil. 2. In a large bowl, combine the almond flour, cocoa powder, baking powder, sweetener, and salt. Add the butter, eggs, and vanilla. Stir until thoroughly combined (the batter will be thick.) Spread the batter into the prepared pan and scatter the chocolate chips on top. 3. Air fry for 15 to 20 minutes until the edges are set (the center should still appear slightly undercooked.) Let cool completely before slicing. To store, cover and refrigerate the brownies for up to 3 days.

Orange Gooey Butter Cake

Prep time: 5 minutes | Cook time: 1 hour 25 minutes | Serves 6 to 8

Crust Layer:

30 g All-purpose flour	60 g unsalted butter, melted
40 g granulated sugar	
½ teaspoon baking powder	1 egg
	1 teaspoon orange extract
⅛ teaspoon salt	2 tablespoons orange zest

Gooey Butter Layer:

230 g cream cheese, softened	2 teaspoons orange extract
110 g unsalted butter, melted	2 tablespoons orange zest
	300 g icing sugar
2 eggs	

Garnish:

Icing sugar	Orange slices

1. Preheat the air fryer to 180ºC. 2. Grease a cake pan and line the bottom with baking paper. Combine the flour, sugar, baking powder and salt in a bowl. Add the melted butter, egg, orange extract and orange zest. Mix well and press this mixture into the bottom of the greased cake pan. Lower the pan into the basket using an aluminum foil sling (fold a piece of aluminum foil into a strip about 2-inches wide by 24-inches long). Fold the ends of the aluminum foil over the top of the dish before returning the basket to the air fryer. Air fry uncovered for 8 minutes. 3. Make the gooey butter layer: Beat the cream cheese, melted butter, eggs, orange extract and orange zest in a large bowl using an electric hand mixer. Add the icing sugar in stages, beat until smooth with each addition. Pour this mixture on top of the baked crust in the cake pan. Wrap the pan with a piece of greased aluminum foil, tenting the top of the foil to leave a little room for the cake to rise. 4. Air fry for 60 minutes. Remove the aluminum foil and air fry for an additional 17 minutes. 5. Let the cake cool inside the pan for at least 10 minutes. Then, run a butter knife around the cake and let the cake

cool completely in the pan. When cooled, run the butter knife around the edges of the cake again and invert it onto a plate and then back onto a serving platter. Sprinkle the icing sugar over the top of the cake and garnish with orange slices.

Shortcut Spiced Apple Butter

Prep time: 5 minutes | Cook time: 1 hour | Makes 1¼ cups

Cooking spray	½ teaspoon kosher, or coarse sea salt
500 g store-bought unsweetened applesauce	¼ teaspoon ground cinnamon
90 g packed light brown sugar	⅛ teaspoon ground allspice
3 tablespoons fresh lemon juice	

1. Spray a cake pan with cooking spray. Whisk together all the ingredients in a bowl until smooth, then pour into the greased pan. Set the pan in the air fryer and bake at 170°C until the apple mixture is caramelized, reduced to a thick purée, and fragrant, about 1 hour. 2. Remove the pan from the air fryer, stir to combine the caramelized bits at the edge with the rest, then let cool completely to thicken. Scrape the apple butter into a jar and store in the refrigerator for up to 2 weeks.

Simple Apple Turnovers

Prep time: 10 minutes | Cook time: 10 minutes | Serves 4

1 apple, peeled, quartered, and thinly sliced	1 tablespoon granulated sugar
½ teaspoons pumpkin pie spice	Pinch of kosher, or coarse sea salt
Juice of ½ lemon	6 sheets filo pastry

1. Preheat the air fryer to 160°C. 2. In a medium bowl, combine the apple, pumpkin pie spice, lemon juice, granulated sugar, and kosher salt. 3. Cut the filo pastry sheets into 4 equal pieces and place individual tablespoons of apple filling in the center of each piece, then fold in both sides and roll from front to back. 4. Spray the air fryer basket with nonstick cooking spray, then place the turnovers in the basket and bake for 10 minutes or until golden brown. 5. Remove the turnovers from the air fryer and allow to cool on a wire rack for 10 minutes before serving.

Strawberry Scone Shortcake

Prep time: 10 minutes | Cook time: 20 minutes | Serves 4 to 6

90 g All-purpose flour	315 ml heavy cream, chilled
3 tablespoons granulated sugar	Turbinado (raw cane) sugar, for sprinkling
1½ teaspoons baking powder	2 tablespoons icing sugar, plus more for dusting
1 teaspoon kosher, or coarse sea salt	½ teaspoon vanilla extract
8 tablespoons unsalted butter, cubed and chilled	165 g quartered fresh strawberries

1. In a large bowl, whisk together the flour, granulated sugar, baking powder, and salt. Add the butter and use your fingers to break apart the butter pieces while working them into the flour mixture, until pea-size pieces form. Pour 155 ml of the cream over the flour mixture and, using a rubber spatula, mix the ingredients together until just combined. 2. Transfer the dough to a work surface and form into a 7-inch-wide disk. Brush the top with water, then sprinkle with some turbinado sugar. Using a large metal spatula, transfer the dough to the air fryer and bake at 180°C until golden brown and fluffy, about 20 minutes. Let cool in the air fryer basket for 5 minutes, then turn out onto a wire rack, right-side up, to cool completely. 3. Meanwhile, in a bowl, beat the remaining 155 ml of cream, the icing sugar, and vanilla until stiff peaks form. Split the scone like a hamburger bun and spread the strawberries over the bottom. Top with the whipped cream and cover with the top of the scone. Dust with icing sugar and cut into wedges to serve.

Desserts | 71

Halle Berries-and-Cream Cobbler

Prep time: 10 minutes | Cook time: 25 minutes | Serves 4

340 g cream cheese, softened	unsalted butter, cut into pieces
1 large egg	¼ teaspoon fine sea salt
40 g powdered sweetener	Frosting:
½ teaspoon vanilla extract	55 g cream cheese, softened
¼ teaspoon fine sea salt	
120 g sliced fresh raspberries or strawberries	1 tablespoon powdered sweetener
Biscuits:	1 tablespoon unsweetened, unflavoured almond milk or heavy cream
3 large egg whites	
35 g blanched almond flour	
1 teaspoon baking powder	Fresh raspberries or strawberries, for garnish
2½ tablespoons very cold	

1. Preheat the air fryer to 200°C. Grease a pie pan. 2. In a large mixing bowl, use a hand mixer to combine the cream cheese, egg, and sweetener until smooth. Stir in the vanilla and salt. Gently fold in the raspberries with a rubber spatula. Pour the mixture into the prepared pan and set aside. 3. Make the biscuits: Place the egg whites in a medium-sized mixing bowl or the bowl of a stand mixer. Using a hand mixer or stand mixer, whip the egg whites until very fluffy and stiff. 4. In a separate medium-sized bowl, combine the almond flour and baking powder. Cut in the butter and add the salt, stirring gently to keep the butter pieces intact. 5. Gently fold the almond flour mixture into the egg whites. Use a large spoon or ice cream scooper to scoop out the dough and form it into a 2-inch-wide biscuit, making sure the butter stays in separate clumps. Place the biscuit on top of the raspberry mixture in the pan. Repeat with remaining dough to make 4 biscuits. 6. Place the pan in the air fryer and bake for 5 minutes, then lower the temperature to 160°C and bake for another 17 to 20 minutes, until the biscuits are golden brown. 7. While the cobbler cooks, make the frosting: Place the cream cheese in a small bowl and stir to break it up. Add the sweetener and stir. Add the almond milk and stir until well combined. If you prefer a thinner frosting, add more almond milk. 8. Remove the cobbler from the air fryer and allow to cool slightly, then drizzle with the frosting. Garnish with fresh raspberries. 9. Store leftovers in an airtight container in the refrigerator for up to 3 days. Reheat the cobbler in a preheated 180°C air fryer for 3 minutes, or until warmed through.

Glazed Cherry Turnovers

Prep time: 10 minutes | Cook time: 14 minutes per batch | Serves 8

2 sheets frozen puff pastry, thawed	cinnamon
	1 egg, beaten
600 g can premium cherry pie filling	90 g sliced almonds
	70 g icing sugar
2 teaspoons ground	2 tablespoons milk

1. Roll a sheet of puff pastry out into a square that is approximately 10-inches by 10-inches. Cut this large square into quarters. 2. Mix the cherry pie filling and cinnamon together in a bowl. Spoon ¼ cup of the cherry filling into the center of each puff pastry square. Brush the perimeter of the pastry square with the egg wash. Fold one corner of the puff pastry over the cherry pie filling towards the opposite corner, forming a triangle. Seal the two edges of the pastry together with the tip of a fork, making a design with the tines. Brush the top of the turnovers with the egg wash and sprinkle sliced almonds over each one. Repeat these steps with the second sheet of puff pastry. You should have eight turnovers at the end. 3. Preheat the air fryer to 190°C. 4. Air fry two turnovers at a time for 14 minutes, carefully turning them over halfway through the cooking time. 5. While the turnovers are cooking, make the glaze by whisking the icing sugar and milk together in a small bowl until smooth. Let the glaze sit for a minute so the sugar can absorb the milk. If the consistency is still too thick to drizzle, add a little more milk, a drop at a time, and stir until smooth. 6. Let the cooked cherry turnovers sit for at least 10 minutes. Then drizzle the glaze over each turnover in a zigzag motion. Serve warm or at room temperature.

Chocolate Peppermint Cheesecake

Prep time: 5 minutes | Cook time: 18 minutes | Serves 6

Crust:

110 g butter, melted	sweetener
30 g coconut flour	Cooking spray
2 tablespoons granulated	

Topping:

110 g unsweetened cooking chocolate	1 teaspoon vanilla extract
180 g mascarpone cheese, at room temperature	2 drops peppermint extract

1. Preheat the air fryer to 180°C. Lightly coat a baking pan with cooking spray. 2. In a mixing bowl, whisk together the butter, flour, and sweetener until well combined. Transfer the mixture to the prepared baking pan. 3. Place the baking pan in the air fryer and bake for 18 minutes until a toothpick inserted in the center comes out clean. 4. Remove the crust from the air fryer to a wire rack to cool. 5. Once cooled completely, place it in the freezer for 20 minutes. 6. When ready, combine all the ingredients for the topping in a small bowl and stir to incorporate. 7. Spread this topping over the crust and let it sit for another 15 minutes in the freezer. 8. Serve chilled.

Cream-Filled Sandwich Cookies

Prep time: 8 minutes | Cook time: 8 minutes | Makes 8 cookies

Coconut, or avocado oil, for spraying	60 ml milk
1 tube croissant dough	8 Oreos
	1 tablespoon icing sugar

1. Line the air fryer basket with baking paper, and spray lightly with oil. 2. Unroll the dough and cut it into 8 triangles. Lay out the triangles on a work surface. 3. Pour the milk into a shallow bowl. Quickly dip each cookie in the milk, then place in the center of a dough triangle. 4. Wrap the dough around the cookie, cutting off any excess and pinching the edges to seal. You may be able to combine the excess dough to cover additional cookies, if desired. 5. Place the wrapped cookies in the prepared basket, seam-side down, and spray lightly with oil. 6. Bake at 180°C for 4 minutes, flip, spray with oil, and cook for another 3 to 4 minutes, or until puffed and golden brown. 7. Dust with the icing sugar and serve.

Pumpkin Cookie with Cream Cheese Frosting

Prep time: 10 minutes | Cook time: 7 minutes | Serves 6

25 g blanched finely ground almond flour	½ teaspoon vanilla extract
25 g powdered sweetener, divided	½ teaspoon pumpkin pie spice
2 tablespoons butter, softened	2 tablespoons pure pumpkin purée
1 large egg	½ teaspoon ground cinnamon, divided
½ teaspoon unflavoured gelatin	40 g low-carb, sugar-free chocolate chips
½ teaspoon baking powder	85 g full-fat cream cheese, softened

1. In a large bowl, mix almond flour and 25 gsweetener. Stir in butter, egg, and gelatin until combined. 2. Stir in baking powder, vanilla, pumpkin pie spice, pumpkin purée, and ¼ teaspoon cinnamon, then fold in chocolate chips. 3. Pour batter into a round baking pan. Place pan into the air fryer basket. 4. Adjust the temperature to 150°C and bake for 7 minutes. 5. When fully cooked, the top will be golden brown, and a toothpick inserted in center will come out clean. Let cool at least 20 minutes. 6. To make the frosting: mix cream cheese, remaining ¼ teaspoon cinnamon, and remaining 25 g sweetener in a large bowl. Using an electric mixer, beat until it becomes fluffy. Spread onto the cooled cookie. Garnish with additional cinnamon if desired.

Rhubarb and Strawberry Crumble

Prep time: 10 minutes | Cook time: 12 to 17 minutes | Serves 6

250 g sliced fresh strawberries	flour, or All-purpose flour
95 g sliced rhubarb	40 g packed light brown sugar
40 g granulated sugar	½ teaspoon ground cinnamon
30 g quick-cooking oatmeal	3 tablespoons unsalted butter, melted
25 g whole-wheat pastry	

1. Insert the crisper plate into the basket and the basket into the unit. Preheat the unit to 190°C. 2. In a 6-by-2-inch round metal baking pan, combine the strawberries, rhubarb, and granulated sugar. 3. In a medium bowl, stir together the oatmeal, flour, brown sugar, and cinnamon. Stir the melted butter into this mixture until crumbly. Sprinkle the crumble mixture over the fruit. 4. Once the unit is preheated, place the pan into the basket. 5.Bake for 12 minutes then check the crumble. If the fruit is bubbling and the topping is golden brown, it is done. If not, resume cooking. 6. When the cooking is complete, serve warm.

Indian Toast and Milk

Prep time: 10 minutes | Cook time: 20 minutes | Serves 4

305 g sweetened, condensed milk	1 pinch saffron threads
240 ml evaporated milk	4 slices white bread
240 ml single cream	2 to 3 tablespoons ghee or butter, softened
1 teaspoon ground cardamom, plus additional for garnish	2 tablespoons crushed pistachios, for garnish (optional)

1. In a baking pan, combine the condensed milk, evaporated milk, half-and-half, cardamom, and saffron. Stir until well combined. 2. Place the pan in the air fryer basket. Set the air fryer to 180°C for 15 minutes, stirring halfway through the cooking time. Remove the sweetened milk from the air fryer and set aside. 3. Cut each slice of bread into two triangles. Brush each side with ghee. Place the bread in the air fryer basket. Keeping the air fryer on 180°C cook for 5 minutes or until golden brown and toasty. 4. Remove the bread from the air fryer. Arrange two triangles in each of four wide, shallow bowls. Pour the hot milk mixture on top of the bread and let soak for 30 minutes. 5. Garnish with pistachios if using, and sprinkle with additional cardamom.

Pineapple Galette

Prep time: 15 minutes | Cook time: 40 minutes | Serves 2

¼ medium-size pineapple, peeled, cored, and cut crosswise into ¼-inch-thick slices	lime
	1 store-bought sheet puff pastry, cut into an 8-inch round
2 tablespoons dark rum, or apple juice	3 tablespoons granulated sugar
1 teaspoon vanilla extract	2 tablespoons unsalted butter, cubed and chilled
½ teaspoon kosher, or coarse sea salt	Coconut ice cream, for serving
Finely grated zest of ½	

1. In a small bowl, combine the pineapple slices, rum, vanilla, salt, and lime zest and let stand for at least 10 minutes to allow the pineapple to soak in the rum. 2. Meanwhile, press the puff pastry round into the bottom and up the sides of a cake pan and use the tines of a fork to dock the bottom and sides. 3. Arrange the pineapple slices on the bottom of the pastry in a more or less single layer, then sprinkle with the sugar and dot with the butter. Drizzle with the leftover juices from the bowl. Place the pan in the air fryer and bake at 150°C until the pastry is puffed and golden brown and the pineapple is lightly caramelized on top, about 40 minutes. 4. Transfer the pan to a wire rack to cool for 15 minutes. Unmold the galette from the pan and serve warm with coconut ice cream.

Bourbon Bread Pudding

Prep time: 10 minutes | Cook time: 20 minutes | Serves 4

3 slices whole grain bread, cubed	½ teaspoons vanilla extract
1 large egg	4 tablespoons maple syrup, divided
240 ml whole milk	½ teaspoons ground cinnamon
2 tablespoons bourbon, or peach juice	2 teaspoons sparkling sugar

1. Preheat the air fryer to 130°C. 2. Spray a baking pan with nonstick cooking spray, then place the bread cubes in the pan. 3. In a medium bowl, whisk together the egg, milk, bourbon, vanilla extract, 3 tablespoons of maple syrup, and cinnamon. Pour the egg mixture over the bread and press down with a spatula to coat all the bread, then sprinkle the sparkling sugar on top and bake for 20 minutes. 4. Remove the pudding from the air fryer and allow to cool in the pan on a wire rack for 10 minutes. Drizzle the remaining 1 tablespoon of maple syrup on top. Slice and serve warm.

Appendix : Recipe Index

A

Air Fried Beef Satay with Peanut Dipping Sauce · 31
Air Fried Butternut Squash with Chopped Hazelnuts · 17
Air Fried Pot Stickers · 55
Almond-Crusted Chicken · 22
Apricot-Glazed Turkey Tenderloin · 26
Asian Glazed Meatballs · 36
Asian Swordfish · 39
Asian-Inspired Roasted Broccoli · 62
Authentic Scotch Eggs · 50
Avocado and Egg Burrito · 11

B

Bacon and Spinach Egg Muffins · 03
Bacon Cheese Egg with Avocado · 04
Bacon Pinwheels · 16
Bacon-Wrapped Pork Tenderloin · 32
Bacon-Wrapped Prawns and Jalapeño Chillies · 53
Bacon, Broccoli and Cheese Bread Pudding · 08
Beef and Tomato Sauce Meatloaf · 32
Beef Jerky · 12
Beef Steak Fingers · 31
Beery and Crunchy Onion Rings · 15
Beetroot Salad with Lemon Vinaigrette · 17
Berry Cheesecake · 11
Black Bean and Tomato Chilli · 66
Bourbon Bread Pudding · 75
Bourbon Vanilla French Toast · 03
Broccoli-Mushroom Frittata · 08
Bruschetta Chicken · 20
Bruschetta with Basil Pesto · 50
Buffalo Egg Cups · 04
Bulgogi Burgers · 36
Butter and Garlic Fried Cabbage · 61
Buttery Sweet Potatoes · 16

C

Cauliflower Rice-Stuffed Peppers · 68
Cheddar Soufflés · 06
Cheese Wine Pork Loin · 30
Cheese-Stuffed Blooming Onion · 51
Cheesy Cabbage Wedges · 67
Cheesy Jalapeño Cornbread · 15
Cheesy Potato Patties · 15

Cheesy Tuna Patties · 41
Chicken Manchurian · 24
Chicken Wings with Piri Piri Sauce · 25
Chilean Sea Bass with Olive Relish · 40
Chinese-Inspired Spareribs · 13
Chocolate Peppermint Cheesecake · 73
Churro Bites · 12
Classic British Breakfast · 07
Classic Spring Rolls · 54
Cod Tacos with Mango Salsa · 45
Coriander Lime Chicken Thighs · 23
Corn Croquettes · 60
Corn Fritters · 18
Cornmeal-Crusted Trout Fingers · 39
Courgette and Spinach Croquettes · 66
Courgette Feta Roulades · 55
Courgette Fritters · 58
Crab Cakes · 41
Crab-Stuffed Avocado Boats · 41
Cranberry Curry Chicken · 26
Cream-Filled Sandwich Cookies · 73
Crispy Aubergine Slices with Parsley · 66
Crispy Duck with Cherry Sauce · 23
Crispy Filo Artichoke Triangles · 55
Crispy Garlic Sliced Aubergine · 63
Crispy Lemon Artichoke Hearts · 61
Crunchy Air Fried Cod Fillets · 44
Crunchy Chicken Tenders · 21
Crunchy Chicken with Roasted Carrots · 20
Crunchy Fried Okra · 16
Crustless Prawn Quiche · 43

D

Double Chocolate Brownies · 70

E

Easy Chicken Fingers · 27
Easy Roasted Asparagus · 18
Easy Sausage Pizza · 08
Egg in a Hole · 05
Egg Tarts · 05

F

Fish and Vegetable Tacos · 11

Fish Cakes · 43
Fish Croquettes with Lemon-Dill Aioli · 40
Fish Tacos with Jalapeño-Lime Sauce · 44
Five-Spice Pork Belly · 33
Fried Asparagus · 63
Fried Brussels Sprouts · 63
Fried Catfish Fillets · 39

G

Garlic and Thyme Tomatoes · 64
Garlic Butter Prawns Scampi · 47
Garlic Courgette and Red Peppers · 58
Garlic-Parmesan Crispy Baby Potatoes · 60
Glazed Cherry Turnovers · 72
Glazed Sweet Potato Bites · 62
Gold Artichoke Hearts · 62
Golden Avocado Tempura · 03
Greek Lamb Rack · 35
Green Eggs and Ham · 04
Gyro Breakfast Patties with Tzatziki · 06

H

Halle Berries-and-Cream Cobbler · 72
Hazelnut Butter Cookies · 70
Herbed Prawns Pita · 46
Hole in One · 02
Homemade Sweet Potato Chips · 53
Homemade Toaster Pastries · 02

I

Indian Aubergine Bharta · 64
Indian Toast and Milk · 74
Italian Baked Egg and Veggies · 66
Italian Chicken Thighs · 21
Italian Chicken with Sauce · 24
Italian Egg Cups · 04
Italian Lamb Chops with Avocado Mayo · 33

J

Jalapeño and Bacon Breakfast Pizza · 02
Jerk Chicken Thighs · 24

K

Kale and Potato Nuggets · 02
Kale Chips with Sesame · 49
Kielbasa Sausage with Pineapple and Peppers · 31

L

Lamb Chops with Horseradish Sauce · 30
Lebanese Muhammara · 52
Lemon Chicken with Garlic · 23
Lemon Pork with Marjoram · 29
Lemon Prawns with Garlic Olive Oil · 50
Lettuce-Wrapped Turkey and Mushroom Meatballs · 26
Loaded Cauliflower Steak · 67

M

Maple-Roasted Tomatoes · 60
Mashed Sweet Potato Tots · 59
Meatball Subs · 12
Mediterranean Air Fried Veggies · 68
Meringue Cookies · 12
Mexican Corn in a Cup · 58
Mexican Pork Chops · 31
Minute Steak Roll-Ups · 30
Mozzarella Cheese Arancini · 51

O

One-Pot Prawn Fried Rice · 46
Onion Pakoras · 53
Orange Gooey Butter Cake · 70

P

Pancake for Two · 09
Panko Pork Chops · 33
Parmesan Herb Filet Mignon · 35
Parmesan-Thyme Butternut Squash · 59
Parsnip Fries with Romesco Sauce · 59
Pecan Rolls · 13
Pecan Turkey Cutlets · 27
Pepperoni Pizza Dip · 51
Peppery Chicken Meatballs · 52
Personal Cauliflower Pizzas · 21
Pineapple Galette · 74
Pork Medallions with Endive Salad · 29
Pork Rind Fried Chicken · 20
Potatoes Lyonnaise · 06
Pumpkin Cookie with Cream Cheese Frosting · 73

Q

Quiche-Stuffed Peppers · 68

R

Rhubarb and Strawberry Crumble · 74

Ritzy Skirt Steak Fajitas	34
Roasted Aubergine	63
Roasted Grape Dip	52
Roasted Halibut Steaks with Parsley	45
Roasted Vegetable Mélange with Herbs	67
Rosemary-Garlic Shoestring Fries	54
Rumaki	55

S

Salmon Spring Rolls	42
Sausage-Stuffed Mushroom Caps	61
Scalloped Veggie Mix	18
Sea Bass with Potato Scales	45
Sea Salt Potato Crisps	52
Shortcut Spiced Apple Butter	71
Simple and Easy Croutons	17
Simple Apple Turnovers	71
Simple Pea Delight	15
Snapper with Shallot and Tomato	40
Soft white cheese Stuffed Jalapeño Chillies Poppers	49
Sole and Cauliflower Fritters	46
South Indian Fried Fish	42
Southwestern Roasted Corn	58
Spanish Chicken and Mini Sweet Pepper Baguette	22
Spicy Chicken Bites	54
Spicy Lamb Sirloin Chops	36
Spicy Tortilla Chips	49
Spinach and Beef Braciole	35
Spinach and Swiss Frittata with Mushrooms	07
Spinach Cheese Casserole	67

Steak, Broccoli, and Mushroom Rice Bowls	32
Strawberry Scone Shortcake	71
Strawberry Tarts	05
Swedish Meatloaf	34
Sweet and Crispy Roasted Pearl Onions	60
Sweet Chili Spiced Chicken	25
Sweet Corn and Carrot Fritters	17

T

Tandoori Prawns	43
Teriyaki Chicken Thighs with Lemony Snow Peas	22
Thai Prawn Skewers with Peanut Dipping Sauce	42
Tofu Bites	61
Tomato and Cheddar Rolls	07
Traditional Queso Fundido	16
Tuna Avocado Bites	41
Turkey Burger Sliders	49
Turkey Meatloaf	27
Turkish Chicken Kebabs	25
Turnip Fries	62

V

Veggie Salmon Nachos	53
Veggie Tuna Melts	11

W

White Bean–Oat Waffles	03

Printed in Great Britain
by Amazon